99 Stories to Start Speeches and Sermons

My thanks go to:

Lester French, also referred to as Mr F

Rev'd Neil Broadbent

And all the saints at

All Saints Church in Kirk Hallam, Derbyshire

And everyone else who has brough humour to my ministry.

99 Stories to Start Speeches and Sermons

Introduction

"Sometimes a smile or to laugh is priceless."

Rev'd Christine French was ordained in the Church of England in 2009, and since then has ministered in a variety of contexts. In this time, she has been asked on numerous occasions for advice about talking in public, from nervous Best Men about their wedding speeches to newly ordained curates who now have the pressure of preaching every week. Humour is not always the answer, but in many times and places it can help.

One thing I've learnt in my time preaching, or speaking at public events is how quickly people can switch off in the first minute of you talking. Hence you generally need something at the start, to engage them, and if they laugh then it shows they are listening. Often it is the funny story that they remember the most, if preaching there is the need to link it into the topic or theme for that day, so they may remember more than the joke you told at the start.

Indeed, one thing I've learnt is how long it can take to think of an amusing (but not offensive) tale or story, hence this collection of 99 such stories have been told by myself when preaching or at other public events. Many are based on my life in the Vicarage with my husband Lester and our assorted cats. Use your discretion to adapt these to what works in your context. The best advice is always make yourself the 'butt' of the joke or story, don't adapt them to insult other people – however tempting it may be, the only person you can laugh at is yourself, then others will laugh along with you.

At best, this book, I hope is a useful resource to help you in your context, and at worse, if it only makes you smile a couple of times, then that's not too bad either.

Index to the Stories

Number	Title
01	Abundance at the Archdeacons Party
02	An Honest Husband
03	Angel Cake
04	Angels in the Gas Meter
05	Baptising Mice
06	Be Careful What You Pray For
07	Beware of the Dog
08	Breakfast at Vicarage
09	Breaking the Toilet
10	Broadband Blues
11	Car Crash on my birthday
12	Chocolate Nativity Story
13	Christmas Presents and Granddad's Hearing
14	College Reunion
15	Crafty Train Ticket
16	Death and Resurrection of Easter Bunny
17	Defying the Aging Process
18	Delayed Plane
19	Dirty Linen
20	Dreams Coming True
21	God is Watching
22	God's Email
23	Grandma's New Hearing Aids
24	Granddads' Christmas Presents
25	Greedy Farmer and God
26	Heaven, a Priest and a Lawyer
27	How to Get to Heaven
28	Husband and Wife arguing in Heaven
29	Keeping the Commandments

30	Lazarus the Goldfish
31	Looking in the Mirror
32	Looking Your Age
33	Mum in the Super Market
34	Noah and the Government
35	Opening the Shop
36	Organist and National Anthem
37	Pessimist and the Light Bulb
38	Phoning the Hospital
39	Presents from the Three Sons
40	Prison Hearing
41	Pub Lunch
42	Rain & the Garden Centre
43	Roller Coaster and Being Scared
44	Salmons Do It
45	Sat Nav Story
46	Smuggling the Unexpected
47	Temptation & Parking
48	The Brick and the Wheelchair
49	The Broken Lawn Mower
50	The Damage of Gossiping
51	The Farmer and the Blind, Old Horse
52	The Farmer, the Horse and the Wake
53	The Fisherman and The Banker
54	The Good Samaritan
55	The Nail Shop
56	The Priest and the Flood
57	The Talkative Turtle
58	The Unused Christmas Present
59	The Wet Present
60	Three Great Kings
61	Three Priests at Conference

62	Three Wise Women at Christmas
63	Top Tips for a Good Marriage
64	Turtle and Young Man
65	Two falcons
66	We Share Everything
67	What a Cow heard
68	Wi-Fi at the Funeral
69	Woman and Frog
70	You've got to keep the worms warm

Additional Stories

71	£86,400
72	Anniversary Gift
73	Bible True or False
74	Bilingual Dog
75	Butterfly and helping
76	Children Writing Nice Things
77	Christmas Cracker Jokes
78	Christmas Day Traditions
79	Christmas Fun Facts
80	Christmas Stamps
81	Conrad the Cockerel
82	Cowboy and the Snake
83	Duggy & Phil working
84	Farming Giving Good Seed
85	Football without a football
86	Get a Wash You Dirty Hippie
87	Hole In One
88	Making Assumptions
89	Our Many Blessings
90	Rat Trap and Helping Others

91	Saint Augustine on the Beach
92	Talking on the Trinity
93	The Parrot and the Burglar
94	The Russian Czar
95	The Talking Dog
96	The Trapped Cat
97	Twins in the Womb
98	What Happens in Heaven
99	What's on TV?

The Main Stories

1. Abundance at the Archdeacon's Party.

Every year Archdeacon Peter kindly held a Supper Party for us curates in his Archdeaconry, and his wife would lay out a fantastic spread of food, it was very kind of them.

I remember the first one my husband Lester and I went to, so impressed with all the choice of food my husband took up the Archdeacon's offer to have more food and he soon went up for seconds, and then thirds. It was when I saw him walking towards me with a fourth plate of food that I snapped and hissed at him "Doesn't it embarrass you that people have seen you go up to the buffet table four times? They are not just going to think of you as being greedy, but also having no manners".

"I'm not a bit bothered" he calmly replied, continuing "I just told them I'm filling the plate up for you!".

> **Notes**: An adaptable little story, you can change the context to your experiences, keeping the theme of a posh dinner party and you being the victim of the joke.

2. An Honest Husband

Getting married late in life did challenge us both – a lot! We had only been married for a few months and I was interviewed on the local news about the Refs 4 Pets charity at Women's Aid, that I supported. We watched the local news together that evening over tea and as I saw myself on the TV screen, I said "Gosh I'm ugly" to which my new husband replied "Yes and you sound common too!"

> **Notes**: Another adaptable little story, have you been on TV, or on a social media video, if not then you could make it generic and suitable for wedding speeches by saying how newlyweds were watching an interview the wife had done on TV and ending with how no-one could ever say that about today's beautiful bride.

3. Angel Cakes

Looking after children is fabulous, but I'm still learning what to say and what not to say, for instance when my 10-year-old niece came to stay when I was living in the countryside. We were walking to the village shop, when she asked about what ingredients went into various products.

So, I explained, "Pork comes from pigs and beef comes from cows." Then she asked, "How DO they get the pork from the pig?" So, as a vegetarian and as a Christian, I felt I had to tell her the truth, and explained that they kill the animal to eat its meat. Horrified, in the village shop she stared into the chiller cabinet where the sausages and burgers were and said, "They KILLED a cow to get THIS?"

She could not believe it, and her little heart was broken. Then, so to cheer her up, I suggested we treated ourselves to some cakes. She looked at the packets and holding one up she said "What is this cake called?" I replied, without thinking, "It's an angel cake." Immediately her eyes filled with big tears, and she wailed, "You mean they KILLED an ANGEL to make this?"

> **Notes**: The innocence of children can bring lots of humour, this story can be adapted, the names changed etc. while keeping the flow of the conversation towards the climax about angels.

4. Angels in the Gas Meter

I admit I am a bit gullible and as a child I was no different, one example being my pocket money. Every week my dad would give me a shiny 50p coin and tell me if I was to spend it, then it would be gone, but if I was to put it into the special red box then it would make the angels smile in heaven.

I dutifully did this for several months, then got bored with making angels smile, preferring to spend my pocket money on sweets. It was in recent years as an adult I was recalling the story with my elder sister only to be told that special red box – wasn't a link to heaven, rather it was the gas meter!

> **Notes**: An amusing innocent child story, I'm aware that such gas meters don't exist anymore, hence you may need to adapt this story depending on your age, you could say "Your grandmother remembered…."

5. Baptising Mice

Three Vicars were having lunch together at a local pub. The first Vicar said, "Do you know, since started in the summer I've been having trouble with mice in my church. I've tried everything--noise, spray, even my cats have come into church, but nothing seems to scare them away."

The second Vicar then said "Yes, me too. I've got dozens of mice living in the crypt of the church. I've set traps and even called an expert to get rid of them, yet they still won't go away."

With a grin on his face, the third Vicar said, "I had the same problem, so I baptized all mine and made them members of the church. I haven't seen one back since!"

> **Notes**: Even though this story is based in a church, it could be related to any group with a membership, i.e. the Rotary Club, a golf club, Women's Institute etc. where by it could be the post holders in similar clubs complaining and third party could say rather than 'baptising' the mice, they could say they've made the mice committee members and never seen them again.

6. Be Careful What You Pray For

I remember when I wanted to change jobs, to help me get more experience in a certain area. Time became very precious in my life, so I prayed for God to help me. God does listen, and within 6 months I was taking voluntary redundancy from my career and able to look for another post. I prayed asking God for a new job – but I had certain criteria, it had to be close to home, as I didn't drive, it had to fit in around my other commitments and the new team had to be fun to work with. That following week I saw the job of my dreams, applied for it, got the interviewed and was hired. I loved it.

It wasn't until I got my first wage packet and saw the drop in my income from my previous salary that I realised, in all my prayers and dealings with God I'd forgot to ask about the hourly rate – so my experience is, be very careful for what you pray for – because God is listening, and God does answer!

> **Notes**: Yes there is a religious element to this story, about praying, which is central to the humour, hence if you do not pray, then maybe you could be talking about a friend, but it looses something in the context.

7. Beware of the Dog

Upon entering the little village shop store, I noticed a sign saying; 'DANGER! BEWARE OF DOG!' posted on the shop door. Inside I noticed a harmless little, old dog asleep on the floor besides the cash register. I asked the shop keeper, "Is THAT the dog folks are supposed to beware of?"

"Yes, that's him," he replied. I couldn't help but be amused. "That certainly doesn't look like a dangerous dog to me, my cats are bigger than your old dog. Why in the world would you post that sign?"

"Because," the owner replied, "before I put up the sign, people kept tripping over him."

> **Notes**: A quaint and amusing little story that can be adapted to your local context.

8. Breakfast at the Vicarage

Last week, I decided to cook breakfast for me and my husband – a rare treat us both being together on a Sunday morning. But it didn't go quite as I planned. He rushed into the kitchen. "Careful," he said, "CAREFUL! Put in some more butter! Oh no! You're cooking too many mushrooms at once. TOO MANY! Turn them! Quickly TURN THEM NOW! We need more butter."

Calmly I replied it was ok, and everything was in hand, to which he replied "Oh no – don't let the eggs over cook! Slow down. They're going to STICK!"

"No they aren't" I replied, going on to say "I have cooked breakfast before."

"Careful" he continued at speed, "the toast is burning and the beans are sticking. CAREFUL! I said be CAREFUL! You NEVER listen to me when you're cooking!"

I stood there, flabbergasted and asked "What in the world is wrong with you? Don't you think know how to cook a breakfast?"

To which my husband calmly replied, "I just wanted to show you what it feels like when you are sat in the passenger seat and I'm driving."

> **Notes**: Men seem to laugh more at this than women! You can adapt this to your context, maybe an evening meal rather than breakfast, what ever is most appropriate for your setting, also I do tell my husband when I am using these stories as people have asked him about it.

9. Breaking the Toilet

My husband is a practical man, which is very hand, he's also a bit of a rough diamond, and renowned for the vocabulary he uses!

It was one Sunday afternoon I heard him shouting and swearing in the Vicarage kitchen – the u-bend had come off the sink and there was water over the floor. I calmed things down by suggesting I could clean up the mess if he could fix the plumbing – which he duly did. Problem solved.

Hence I was a little surprised the next morning, while I was lying in bed to hear him shouting and swearing again. I went down to the kitchen fearing the worse, only to find it clean and tidy. So I went back to bed, and five minutes later Mr F popped his head around the door saying he was off out to work.

"What was all that swearing about?" I asked, and he replied "I dropped my mug in the toilet and it broke".

"Well, that's nothing to get worked up about" I replied, continuing 'it's only a mug, we've got shelves full of them".

To which he clarified "no not the mug, the toilet, the basin broke and there's water all over the bathroom floor!"

Notes: Characters and contexts can be altered as appropriate, it's the surprise twist at the end, that dropping a mug in a toilet breaks the toilet rather than the mug!

10.   Broadband Blues

There was trouble in our household at the start of the week. Communication was rather strained, in fact it just wasn't happening. Well one was communicating to the other, but the other just wasn't listening – properly!

As one day went into another it began to make me rather anxious, stressed and then I just got angry with the whole situation. I'm aware it takes a lot of effort to repair things. I just was going round in circles and then getting annoyed with everyone and everything. I knew I needed to do something about the problem. So, I made myself a mug of tea, sat down and phoned for guidance and support – and yes I made the phone call I dreaded, but many of us here might have to make at some point – I phone the Broadband Help line saying "Please can you help me – my internet isn't talking to my computer".

Well John, Ann and Helen couldn't help me but eventually, the following day I spoke to Gary – for nearly two hours, as he worked out how to fix things. While we were waiting for the computer to restart for the umpteenth time, we chatted and I explained what I did for a living and how normally at the start of the week I'd try to get most of my sermon notes done for the forthcoming Sunday.

"What's the topic this week?" he asked, feeling pleasantly surprised by his interest I told him that it was the Healing Service, to which he chatted about healing computers and the stress they cause so many people. He's right, it had made me grumpy and stressed. But why? Computers are great when they work, but when they don't it does get very stressful quickly!

> **Notes**: It's building up in the initial start of the story about how bad the communications situation in your household was, so people will assume its you and your partner who have fallen out, hence the surprise or twist when it's the computer and internet. You can end the story there, or carry on with the second paragraph if you can make it relevant (and ironic) to what you were doing and getting stressed about.

11.   Car Crash on My Birthday

It was on my birthday a few years ago I was getting ready to do an assembly in a local school, and on the table in the front room was my present from my loving husband – a plant, you know when you walk into supermarket and see their plants, it was one of them, well actually it was two because they were on offer.

Anyhow my husband said he would make it up to me and take me out for lunch. I explained to him how I needed to nip into Derby to get some baptism supplies from the Cathedral shop. So, it was agreed and after the assembly, still wearing my clergy collar, we left for Derby. Now before marriage no one explained to me that when going out it is the man who drives to the pub and the woman who drives back.

As Mr F drove us to Derby, we were at the junction to turn onto the A52, when suddenly our car was hit from behind by another car. Well I looked at Mr F and the first words that came out of my mouth, weren't 'are you ok' but rather "Don't hit anyone!".

He jumped out the car to inspect the damage, and I too got out dreading the confrontation. Well, the other driver, he looked at 6 foot 5 inches tall Mr F, then looked across at me, still wearing my dog collar and I'm not sure if it was the fear of God or the fear of my husband but he put his hands up in the air apologising, saying "It's 100% my fault".

Notes: This can be adapted to other contexts, the contract between the fear of a tall aggressive man and a peaceful priest often creates some interesting stories.

12. Chocolate Nativity Story

At Christmas time, one story you will hear many times is that of the Nativity. But we don't always remember it, so I'd now like to re-tell this Christmas story – but with a few props to help us to remember this amazing story….so who likes chocolates….well you may like this story…

As you know it all began with a girl called Mary who heard a WISPA, from an angel who told her that she would give birth to God's son. But how could this be? She was not yet married to Joseph. To have a baby now would be real TOPIC of conversation in the village. But in a dream, Joseph also heard of God's plan and decided he had to wanted to be obedient to God.

But before the baby arrived, political events overtook them. Joseph had to return to Bethlehem for the census - it was miles away - a long, long journey, but Joseph thought the BREAK-A-WAY would do Mary good. They had to travel on a donkey simply because in those days they couldn't get an AEROplane, or a DOUBLE DECKER. When they arrived, Joseph tried to find lodgings, but they tried CLUB after CLUB but they were turned them away. "No room", they all said.

Eventually they were offered a small stable - it was there that the baby was born. He was named Jesus, which means Saviour. And as the baby slumbered, his mother gazed lovingly at her baby while keeping her warm, in her lap slept a little KIT KAT.

That night, some shepherds, in nearby fields heard angelic noises in the sky, and so beautiful was their singing, some nearby MINISTRELS joined in singing "Glory to God in the Highest".

The shepherds decided to take some TIME-OUT from their sheep, to go and see what's happening in Bethlehem. When they got there they found Joseph, and Mary and Jesus, who was lying in a manger of all places – certainly no bed of a king or a bed of ROSES! But they were united in wonder, and they REVELled in the thought that this child was so special and they, the shepherds were his first visitors. Could this be little baby be the one the prophets had foretold - was he the LION of Judah? But it was getting late, AFTER EIGHT, in fact - so the shepherds returned to the hills – with joy in their hearts and singing praise to God as they went.

Meanwhile in a far country, there were some Wise men – many people called them SMARTIES - who were busily scanning the GALAXY and observing the stars, when they saw a new light in the MILKY WAY. Could it be MARS? No, it was a special star - signalling the birth of a King. They realised that if they didn't get moving, they would soon be out of TIME. They knew they were meant to follow the star, so they packed a PICNIC, did up their BUTTONS and climbed on their camels.

A few days later, on the way to their destination, they went to Herod's Palace - not afraid to HOBNOB with royalty - to see if Herod knew about this royal birth. Herod was very interested - "A King has been born?" he was worried and tried to FUDGE the issue by saying that he wanted to go and worship the baby as well - and told the wise men to report to him on their way back.

The wise men set off and eventually found the young Jesus and they offered him all their BOUNTY - Gold, Frankincense, and some Myrrh. Then God warned them in a dream that Herod was up to no good and they should not return back to him, rather they found another way home, this was the ROCKY route.

Now that's just a few HIGHLIGHTS from the familiar story told at Christmas. The important thing to remember is not the chocolates but according to the Bible, Jesus was born so that ALLSORTS of people might come know God's love for them. Like the shepherds and the Wise men, many people are looking for meaning and purpose - some kind of BOOST in life – and having Jesus in our lives, not just at Christmas but every day is a real cause for CELEBRATION'S! Amen to that!

Notes: I've used this several times at Midnight Mass, walking through the church and giving out the relevant sweets/chocolates to random members of the congregation – it is getting increasingly expensive to do so. Hence you might want to do it with pictures of the relevant chocolates or even to have it as a game of bingo for the work's Christmas Party.

13.   Christmas Presents and Granddad's Hearing

My two young nephews were spending the night at their grandparents the week before Christmas. At bedtime, the two boys knelt beside their beds to say their prayers when the youngest one began praying at the top of his lungs.

"I PRAY FOR A NEW BICYCLE! AND AN XBOX 360! AND I PRAY FOR THE NEW IRON MAN COMIC BOOK!"

His older brother leaned over and nudged the younger brother and said, "Why are you shouting your prayers? God isn't deaf."

To which the little brother replied, "No, but Granddad is!"

> **Notes**. This quaint little story can be adapted to your particular context, changing genders, toys requested and changing who the older relative is too.

14.   College Reunion

It was twenty years since I'd left college and I was looking forward to the reunion despite travelling in the cold winter weather. My husband came along too, and noticed I was staring rather a lot at a very drunk man, staggering around the room. "Do you know him?" he bluntly asked.

"Yes" I sighed "He's my old boyfriend. I've been told he took to drinking after we split up all those years ago, and I hear he's hardly been sober since".

"My God" my husband exclaimed "who would have thought a person could go on celebrating that long?"

It was a frosty journey back home that night!

> **Notes:** We all have pasts and carry emotional baggage, sometimes a little joke or funny story can help heal.

15.   Crafty Train Tickets

On our way to a conference, I and two other Anglican priests were buying train tickets. I couldn't help but notice the three Methodist minister next to us, going to the same conference, only bought one ticket.

"How are three people going to travel on only one ticket?" I asked with innocence and annoyance.

"Watch and you'll see," answered one of the young ministers as we all boarded the train. We priests got seats around a table but the three ministers all crammed into a toilet and closed the door behind them. Shortly after the train departed, the conductor came around collecting tickets. He knocked on the restroom door and said, "Ticket, please".

Under the door a single ticket poked out, the conductor stamped it and moved on. We saw this and agreed it was a quite clever idea. So, after the conference, we Anglican priests decide to copy the Methodist ministers on the return trip and save some money (being clever with money, and all that). When we got to the station, they bought a single ticket for the return trip. To my astonishment, the Methodists didn't buy a ticket at all.

"How are you going to ride without a ticket?" I asked.

"Watch and you'll see", answered one of them. When they boarded the train, the three Methodist ministers crammed into a toilet and we did the same on the other side of the aisle. The train departed. Shortly afterwards there was a knock on our toilet door saying "Ticket, please" to which we dutifully pushed under the door the one ticket and thought how clever we were. Until I realised I recognised the voice, it was the young Methodist minister – he'd got our ticket!

Notes. This was more relevant before trains had automatic doors and were opposite each other at the end of the carriage. Despite the practicalities it's a fun way of showing how gullible you can be, also the roles, or denominations can be changed as relevant to your context – ideally another group that you have a gentle rivalry with i.e. different football teams that can be clearly seen as a member of that group.

---

16.   **Death and Resurrection of the Easter Bunny**

A man was blissfully driving along the ring road, when he saw the Easter Bunny hopping across the middle of the road. He swerved to avoid hitting the little bunny. Unfortunately, the rabbit jumped in front of his car and was hit. The basket of colourful eggs she had been carrying flew all over the place. Easter Eggs were scattered everywhere.

The driver, being a sensitive man as well as an animal lover, pulled over to the side of the road and got out to see what had become of the poor little Bunny. Much to his dismay, the colourful Bunny was dead. The driver felt guilty and he began to cry.

A woman driving behind him on the ring road slowed down, she saw the man crying on the side of the road and pulled over. She stepped out of her car and asked the man what was wrong.

"I feel terrible," he explained, "I accidentally hit the Easter Bunny and killed it. What should I do?"

The sensible woman told the man not to worry. She knew exactly what to do. She went to her car boot and pulled out a spray can. She walked over to the limp, dead Bunny. Then she sprayed the entire contents of the can onto the little furry animal.

Miraculously the Easter Bunny came to back life. She jumped up, picked up the eggs and sweets, waved her paw at the two humans and hopped on down the road. 50 feet away the Easter Bunny stopped, turned around, waved again. And then she hopped on down the road for about another 50 feet, turned, waved. Then she hopped another 50 feet and waved again! And so it went on as she disappeared into the distance.

The man was astonished, he said to the woman, "What in heaven's name is in your spray can? What was it that you sprayed on the Easter Bunny?"

The wise woman turned the can around, so that the man could read the label. It said: "Hair spray. Restores life to dead hair. And adds permanent wave."

> **Notes**. A classic old story with a few dreadful puns in it. You can alter the story to include local roads to you, and one on occasion I even had a rabbit hand puppet to add extra humour, but then the village I was living in was called Bunny!

17. Defying the Aging Process

A middle-aged woman has a heart attack and is taken to the hospital. While on the operating table she has a near death experience. During that experience she sees God and asks if this is it, is her time on earth ended. God says "no" and explains that she has another 40 years to live.

Upon her recovery she decides to amend her life. She stays in the hospital to have a face lift, liposuction, breast enlargement, tummy tuck, etc. She even has someone come in and change her hair colour. She figures since she's got another 40 years she might as well make the most of it. She walks out of the hospital after the last operation and is killed by an ambulance speeding by. She arrives in front of God and complains, "I thought you said I had another 40 years." God replied, "I didn't recognize you."

> **Notes.** You could change the gender of the person, and what sort of plastic surgery they have to match your own gender.

18. Delayed Plane

I love flying – small or large aeroplanes, helicopters are my favourite and I've even been in a hot air balloon – I just love it. But that wasn't the case of one flight a few years ago, when the plane, after going down the run away, did a U-turn and headed back to the airport and we passengers were sat there for over an hour without any explanation of what had happened. Thankfully we took off without incident, and part way into the journey, when serving refreshments I asked the air steward what had caused the delay, to which he calmly replied "The pilot was bothered by a noise he heard in the engine", going on to add "and it took us a while to find a new pilot."

> **Notes**. A great little twist at the end, you could make a longer story by adding in local details or other relevant experiences.

19.   Dirty Linen

When moving into a Vicarage, I never know what to expect and getting to know our new neighbours can be a bit stressful. I remember after one move, looking through the window and saw a new neighbour, who was hanging out her washing to dry.

"Look at her dirty washing!" I exclaimed to my husband. He just grunted and carried on reading the newspaper.

"Perhaps her soap powder ran out, or the washing machine is broken, after all this is a poor parish, I ought to help her" I suggested.

Over our first week in the Vicarage, every morning I was shocked and disturbed by the various dirty washing she was putting out to dry on the line. Then one morning I nearly screamed in shock "it's clean, thank heavens she must have got a new washing machine".

"No, I don't think so," my husband answered — going on to say, "today I just woke up a little bit earlier and cleaned our windows".

> **Notes.** An amusing way to have the moral element of not judging others.

20. Dreams Come True

It was the week before my birthday, I woke up, startled by a dream, in which my husband had given me a beautiful gold necklace as a birthday present. Over breakfast the following morning I innocently recounted the dream to him, asking "hmm... so what do you think it means?"

To which he mumbled something and replied, "Oh by this time next week I guess you'll have figured it out."

The following week, on my birthday, my eyes opened wide, when on the breakfast table I saw a beautiful gold presentation bag from my husband. Remembering the dream, I carefully, but excitedly open the bag, to find it contained – no, not a gold necklace, rather a book, entitled "The Meaning of Dreams".

> **Notes:** Once again I am the 'butt' of my own stories, obviously you can adapt this nice story to your own names, but it's always advisable to let the other person know what you are going to say they said.

21.　God is Watching

It was the first week at my theology college, and all us students were lined up in the cafeteria for lunch. At the head of the table was a large, tempting stack of fruit. The nun, I'm not sure if it was because we were new, or because of the constant cut backs at the institute, but she wrote a sign and put on the fruit tray saying: "Take only ONE. God is watching."

Moving further along the lunch line, at the other end of the table, I saw an even more tempting plate of cakes, my friends little boy, turned around to me and said "Christine, take all the cakes you want. God's watching the apples."

> **Notes:** A sweet story of the innocence of children and can be adapted to various settings. For a non-faith version, you could change God to the Manager or security camera.

22.　God's Email

It was just before Christmas; God was looking down at Earth and saw all of the evil that was going on. So, God decided to send an angel down to Earth to check it out. God called one of the most devoted of angels and sent the angel to Earth. When she returned, she told God, "Yes, sorry, it is bad on Earth, 95% is bad and only 5% is good."

Well, God thought for a moment and said, "maybe I had better send down a second angel to get another point of view". So, God called another angel and sent her to Earth too. When the angel returned, she went to God and said "Yes, the Earth was in decline, 95% was bad and 5% was good."

God said this was not good. Then God decided to email the 5% that were good and wanted to encourage them, give them a little something to help them keep going. Do you know what that email said?

No? Ah, so you didn't get one either. No, nor did I – hey ho...

> **Notes:** Once again the 'butt' of the joke is the teller of the joke, the unexpected twist that you are not better than anyone else. Rather hard to take out the religious element of this story, but you could try using a CEO rather than God, and consultants rather than angels.

23. Grandma's New Hearing Aids

Have you ever heard anything that wasn't meant for your ears to hear?

I only have a handful of memories of my grandmother, but one is how she was rather deaf, so we had to shout at her. She did get some hearing aids, but it seemed they didn't work, so we all still shouted at her.

I remember in my frustration saying "Grandma, don't your hearing aids work anymore?"

She replied, "Yes, they do a bit", I continued "So can you hear us?"

"Oh yes" she smiled, and then I asked "So if you can hear us, what difference has it made?"

To which she replied "Oh, I've changed my will three times!"

> **Notes:** Sometimes we can underestimate people because they are elderly, again Grandma gets the better of the narrator in this little story. Obviously details can be changed as relevant to the context.

24. Granddad's Christmas Presents

One of the Christmas traditions I hate, is queuing, especially when I'm wasting my time in a shop's queue to give them my money for something I'm going to give to someone else, who probably, after a couple of weeks will have forgotten what I bought them anyway. Last year, while in a long slow queue, I did overhear a lovely conversation, between a granddad and his young grandson, it went a bit like this...

"For Christmas this year I want a new X Box 360 with Connect, and a Toy Story Turbo Glow Buzz Light-year, and a Cars remote control car, and Erik from Happy Feet, he sings and dances, and Stinky the Garbage truck from Matchbox and... and..." well the little boy realised his Granddad had switched off so to get his interest again, he asked his granddad "Granddad – when you were my age, what did you get for Christmas"

The old chap perked up and replied "When I was your age, all I got for Christmas was an apple and an orange".

"Wow" replied the little boy "you got a computer and a mobile phone!"

Notes: I have a feeling the time of Orange as a mobile provider is drifting into the past, hence this lovely story may be to be updated as technology up dates, after all a generation are growing up with raspberry pi(e)' having a different meaning.

---

25.   Greedy Farmer and God

I'd like to share a traditional folk tale from Turkey. This story tells the story of a greedy man who is never satisfied with what he has. The more he gets, the more he wants. So if you are sitting comfortably, then I'll begin. There was a farmer in a village. He was very ambitious. He wanted to make more and more money. In the spring time, when it was rainy, he called out to God, "If it were sunny, I would sow some wheat." The next day, it became sunny, and the farmer sowed some wheat.

After that, he called out to God, "If it were rainy, it would be useful for my wheat." The following day, it rained. The farmer called out to God, "If you gave more rain, my wheat would grow more." The following day, it rained again. Then, in summertime, he harvested his wheat and collected it in a heap. The farmer called out to God, "If you had given more rain, my wheat harvest would have been bigger."

He asked God, "Why didn't you give me more rain and more wheat?" Then God made heavy rain, and all of the farmer's wheat was washed away with the water.

Perhaps we can all learn from the folk tale of the greedy farmer, that we all should be more grateful for what we do have.

> **Notes:** A story with a moral, and often easier said in a story format, hence the traditional (and comfortingly familiar to many) opening of 'If you are sitting comfortably, then I'll begin'.

26.   Heaven, a Priest, and a Lawyer

A young couple were getting excited about their wedding day, just a few weeks away, when their car came off the road, crashing into a tree and both died at the scene of the accident. Immediately they found themselves with Saint Peter in Heaven, and told him how they were so excited about getting married, would it be possible for them to get married in heaven? To which Peter said, he would go find out. He was gone a long time, indeed a very long time, it was several weeks before he joyfully returned to the young couple saying "Yes we can get you married in heaven".

The woman then said she's had time to think about things, and just in case things didn't work out, after all Eternity is a long time, if things didn't work out, could she get a divorce in heaven? At which point Saint Peter looked exasperated and replied, "Look ,it took me weeks to find a priest up here, how much long do you think it's going to take to find a lawyer?"

> **Notes:** If you are a priest, or there is a lawyer in your congregation then that makes this little story far more entertaining. Don't dwell on the sadness of the wedding couple dying, perhaps bringing in a 'panto' feel you could do an exaggerated 'ahh' and ask the congregation/audience to do the same. I wasn't expecting my congregation to laugh out loud about how long it took to find a priest – so be prepared to wait a couple of seconds before saying the final line about the lawyer.

27.   How to Get to Heaven

Before my curacy I'd never worked with children, and not having children of my own, they were a bit of a mystery to me, but they never cease to amaze me. During a recent assembly I said to the children

"If I sold my house and my car, had a big garage sale and gave all my money to the church, would that get me into Heaven?"

"No!" the children all answered.

So then I asked, "So if I cleaned the church every day, mowed the Church yard, and kept everything neat and tidy, would that get me into Heaven?"

Again, the answer was, "No!"

So I continued, feeling a bit more confident that they understood a little about God's kindness and the importance of looking after others less fortunate than us, so I asked "Well, then, if I was kind to animals and gave sweets to all the children, and loved my neighbour, would that get me into Heaven?"

Again, they all answered, "No!"

So more confident that they had an awareness about prayer and worship I asked the children "Well, then how can I get into Heaven?"

To which a little five-year-old boy shouted out, "You gotta be dead!"

True but a bit blunt! I'm learning children speak honestly, and bluntly.

> **Notes:** That innocence from children is charming and sometimes blunt. Again the context could be changed to another group of children i.e. play group, or out with family members etc.

28. Husband and Wife Arguing in Heaven

Have you heard the story about the 80 year old husband and wife, who both died at the very same time? They had lived a frugal, sensible life, worked hard and ate a well-balanced diet.

When they got to heaven, they were astounded by the spectacular beauty they saw there. Lush, rolling lawns, bright fragrant flowers, brilliant sunshine, gentle breezes, and the crowning touch – as far as the man was concerned – the most incredible golf course he had ever seen. It was spectacular! Then the husband had a nasty thought, with disgust, he looked at his wife, and said to her with disdain in his voice

"You! If it weren't for you and all that healthy living, fibre, and bran, we could have been here 20 years ago!"

> **Notes:** Obviously the golf course can be changed as per your context i.e. to 'a lake full of fish' if you were speaking at a gathering of people who fish. Yes the couple are heterosexual, but this could be changed as relevant.

29. Keeping the Commandments

Harold and Jane were not a very religious couple but tried their best; they only came to my church once or twice a year. As they were leaving the church, I said, "Harold, it would be nice to see you and Jane here more than a couple of times year"

"I know," replied Harold, "We're very busy people, leading active lives but at least we keep the Ten Commandments"

"That's great," I replied. "I'm glad to hear that you keep the Commandments."

"Yes, we do" Harold said proudly, "Jane keeps six of them and I keep the other four".

> **Notes:** There is culturally appropriate background knowledge assumed in this story, hence can only really be effective in certain settings i.e. people who will understand what the Ten Commandments are.

30.   Lazarus the Goldfish

"Can you look after my goldfish while I go on holiday?" was the simple request from a friend, "Of course" I replied.

Little did I know that my cats would love lapping up the fishy tasting water, no desire to catch the fish, but loving drinking the water from the tank. When my friend collected her goldfish, I found myself going and buying a tank and a couple of goldfish to keep my cats happy.

So the cats could drink their favourite tipple the tank had no lid. I didn't know then that goldfish can jump and jump out of their tank. Imagine my shock one morning when I found a goldfish had jumped clean out of the tank of water and landed, ironically, below, in, yes, the cats feeding bowl.

I was running late for work and needed to leave to get the bus for work, so on an impulse I tossed the little fish back into the tank, where it floated around on its side, dead to the whole world.

That evening, back from work, I had to face my fears and bury the dead fish – with some dignity. Although pleased to see it was actually swimming around the tank – the fish that was dead was now alive, I was confused. So, the fish was promptly re-named, Lazarus.

> **Notes:** Another story that need the audience (or congregation) to have the knowledge of who the Biblical Lazarus was and what happened to him to make the story work.

31. Looking In The Mirror

Despite various diets, weight loss clubs and gyms, I still felt frustrated about my aging body, and one morning was looking at myself in the mirror, when my husband came into the bedroom and asked what the matter was?

"I feel horrible, I look old and fat, my hair is now just a frizzy grey mess. I really need a compliment" I complained.

To which he quickly replied, "Well your eyesight is perfect".

> **Notes:** If a moral is needed, I think it should be never go fishing for compliments.

32.   Looking Your Age

Now I'm in my mid-fifties, I explained to my husband that the expensive night creams and cosmetics are not a waste of money, but rather an investment in me. After a couple of weeks of using the one that got lots of media hype, I asked him what age I now looked, studying me closely he replied

"From your skin, 21, from your hair 18, from your figure perhaps 25."

Smiling I replied "oh you do flatter me."

"Hang on" he said, "I haven't added them up yet!"

> **Notes:** Of course the names and ages can be changed, the main thing is that the joke was on me.

33.   Mum in the Supermarket

Yesterday I had to nip to the supermarket, and really wished I hadn't. It was so packed, and of course there was a screaming toddler. As mother and daughter passed the freshly baked cakes, the little girl asked for cookies and her mother told her, "No."

To which the little girl immediately began to whine and fuss, and the mother said quietly, "Now Jessica, we just have half of the aisles left to go through - don't be upset. It won't be long now."

Our paths crossed again in the chocolate isle, the child was shouting for chocolate. When her mum said she couldn't have any, she began to cry even more. The mother said, "There, there, Jessica, don't cry - only two more aisles to go and then we'll be at the checkout."

When I got to the checkout - they were in front of me, and of course with the sweets next to the till, the little girl immediately began to clamour for sweets and burst into a terrible tantrum upon discovering there'd be no sweets bought. Her mother said serenely, "Jessica, we'll be through this check out in 5 minutes and then you can go home and have a nice nap."

I ended up walking along side mum and daughter as we walked out of the shop and so I said "I couldn't help noticing and being impressed with how patient you were with little Jessica,"

To which she abruptly replied, "My daughter's name is Tammy, I'm Jessica."

> **Notes:** The names and gender and supermarket can be changed to be more relevant to your own context, but a lovely twist at the end.

34.   Noah and the Government

The Lord spoke to Noah and said: "In six months I'm going to make it rain until the whole earth is covered with water and all the evil people are destroyed. But I want to save a few good people, and two of every kind of living thing on the planet. I am ordering you to build me an ark."

And in a flash of lightning, he delivered the specifications for an ark. "Okay," said Noah, trembling in fear and fumbling with the blueprints. "Six months and it starts to rain". The Lord thundered "You'd better have my ark completed or learn how to swim for a very long time."

Six months passed. The skies began to cloud up and rain began to fall. The Lord saw that Noah was sitting in his front yard, weeping. And there was no ark. "Noah," shouted he Lord, "where is my ark?" as a lightning bolt crashed into the ground next to Noah.

"Lord, please forgive me!" begged Noah. "I did my best, but there were big problems. First I had to get a building permit for the ark construction project, and your plans didn't meet their requirements. So

I had to hire an engineer to redraw the plans." God grumbled - think of the sound of thunder.

Noah carried on "Then I got into a big fight over whether or not the ark needed a fire sprinkler system and the local Fire Safety Inspection Officer had to be contacted. My neighbours objected, claiming I was violating a residential area by building the ark in my front garden, so I had to get a permission from the council for an industrial use."

"Then I had a big problem getting enough wood for the ark because there was a ban on cutting trees to save rare owls. I had to convince the Department for Environment, Food and Rural Affairs that I needed the wood to save the owls. But they wouldn't let me catch any owls. So, no owls."

"Then the carpenters formed a separate union and went out on strike. I had to negotiate a settlement with the unions before anyone would pick up a saw or a hammer. Now we have 6 carpenters going on the boat, and still now owls."

"Then I started gathering up animals and got sued by an animal rights group and the RSPCA got involved. They objected to me taking only two of each kind. Just when I got the case dismissed, the Department of the Environment notified me that I couldn't complete the ark without filing an environmental impact statement on your proposed flood."

God grumbled louder as Noah continued, "They didn't take kindly to the idea that they had no jurisdiction over the conduct of a Supreme Being. Then the Government's Flood Line wanted a map of the proposed new flood plain so they could answer any queries about it. I sent them a globe."

"Right now I'm still trying to resolve a complaint from the Equality and Human Rights Commission over how many foreign labours I'm able to employ. The Inland Revenue and Customs Agency have seized all my assets, claiming I'm trying to avoid paying taxes by leaving the country; and I just got a notice from the state about owing some kind of property tax."

"I really don't think I can finish your ark for at least another five years," Noah wailed.

The sky began to clear. The sun began to shine. A rainbow arched across the sky. Noah looked up and smiled. "You mean you're not going to destroy the earth?" Noah asked, hopefully.

"No," said God sadly, "it seems the Government already has done that."

Notes: Again knowledge about who Noah was is central for the full understanding of this modern twist on an Old Testament story.

35. Opening the Shop

It was the day of the big sale. Rumours of the sale (and some advertising in the local paper) were the main reason for the long line that had formed in front of the shop by 8:30 am, the opening time, and I was nowhere near the front of the queue, but already people were starting to push and jostle each other.

I noticed a small man pushing his way to the front of the line, only to be pushed back, amid loud complaints of queue jumping. On the man's second attempt, he was punched square in the jaw, and knocked around a bit, and then thrown to the end of the line again.

As I watched him get up the second time, I overheard him saying to the person at the end of the line, "That does it! If they hit me one more time, I'm not opening the shop today at all!"

> **Notes:** A short little story to remind us that sometimes things are far wider than what we understand.

36. Organist and the National Anthem

I was Sunday and I was preoccupied with thoughts of how I was going to, ask the congregation to come up with more money towards the repairs to the church building.

Therefore, I was rather annoyed to find that our regular organist was sick and a substitute had been brought in at the last minute. The substitute wanted to know what to play. "Here's a copy of the service," I said impatiently. "But you'll have to think of something to play after I make the announcement about the finances, they won't be happy about it."

So during the service, I paused and said, "Brothers and Sisters, we are in great difficulty; the roof repairs cost twice as much as we expected, and we need £6,000 more. If any of you who can pledge £100 or more, please stand up."

At that moment, the substitute organist played the National Anthem and of course everyone stood up!

And that is how the substitute became the regular organist!

> **Notes:** Asking a congregation for money is never easy, but I do like the organist's style.

37. Pessimist and the Light Bulb

I'm beginning to learn how much of a pessimist my husband is, when recently I asked him to change the light bulb in the porch that had broken. A simple task I thought, but to which he sighed and said that it the old one was so ancient that it looked like it was screwed into too tight, so it might take a while to get it out and it would probably break when he did it. When I nagged him the following day, as he still hadn't done it, he then replied, why bother as it would be a waste of time because these new bulbs aren't made to last, and the new bulb probably won't work either!

However one positive to being married to a pessimist, is when I borrow money off him, he never expects it back – so now I don't give it him back!

> **Notes:** The added extra when I say this is that my husband is actually an electrician who does street lighting as his job. Again I'd suggest changing the characters in this story to make it more relevant to your own context.

38. Phoning the Hospital

Have you ever tried to phone a local hospital to find out how a friend or family member is doing? It's a nightmare! After getting transferred between different wards and departments, being put on hold for ages, then you've got to have their address and date of birth to hand before any information can be shared with you. I hope you find the following story of what a friend did can be of some comfort.

My friend Julie was trying to phone the hospital, and after being passed around various departments and held on hold, eventually she got through to the ward she had asked for, and when the nurse answered she said "Please can you let me know how your patient Julie Smith is? Is she getting any better?"

The nurse on the other end replied, "Please can you tell me her address or date of birth - for data protection reasons" and duly my friend quoted correctly both pieces of information. The nurse then was able to give an update on the patient asked about "Oh, yes. Julie Smith is doing very well. In fact, she's had two full meals, her blood pressure is fine, she's going to be taken off the heart monitor in a couple of hours and if she continues this improvement, the doctor is going to send her home tomorrow."

My friend replied, "Thank God! That's wonderful! That's fantastic! That's such wonderful news!"

The nurse on the phone said, "From your enthusiasm, I take it you must be a close family member or a very close friend!"

And she replied, "Actually I'm Julie Smith and the doctor hasn't told me anything!"

> **Notes:** I'm not keen on having to use a story that is from a different person's experience, but I've never been in hospital, hence one still needs to keep our integrity when telling stories for speeches and sermons. We can exaggerate the truth but if completely fabricating something then to many people it is blatantly obvious.

39. Presents from the Three Sons

Are you sitting comfortably? Then I shall begin. Once upon a time three successful brothers, who all had done well in their lives, decided that now was the time to treat their elderly mother to some luxuries in life as she had done so much for them. A few weeks later they met up and shared what gift they had given their elderly mother.

The first said, "I built a big house for our mother."

The second said, "I sent her a Mercedes with a driver."

The third smiled and said, "You remember how Mum enjoyed reading the Bible? And you know her eyesight is failing. I sent her a remarkable parrot. This parrot recites the entire Bible. It took 12 years to teach him. He's one of a kind. Mum just needs to name the chapter and verse, and the parrot recites it."

Soon thereafter, the gifts arrived and their elderly mother sent out letters of thanks, of a sort:

She wrote one son, "The house you built is so huge. I live in only one room, but I have to clean the whole house."

She wrote to second son, "I am too old to travel. I stay most of the time at home, so I rarely use the Mercedes. And the driver is so rude!"

And finally to the third son , "You had the good sense to know what your mother likes. The chicken was delicious."

> **Notes:** Well, we don't all see everything the same. The sons just didn't understand what their mother really wanted, and this is a quaint story to remind us that even the best plans can easily get mixed up completely.

40. Prison Hearing

While working in the chaplaincy at Nottingham Prison I saw and learnt a lot. The Prison, at that time, had over 500 male prisoners, many of them on remand waiting for trail or sentencing. I soon learnt that they are not all as innocent as they protested, but I also saw a diversity of differ Christian traditions come and lead worship, including the young women from a local free church – who were so popular with the young male inmates that we had to restrict their lay on of hands! The young Christian women just hadn't realised how the prisoners were responding to it!

I'll always remember one Church coming in who specialised in healing. It was during the call to come up, that one prisoner who suffered with slight deafness nervously approached the pastor and explained about his hearing impairment. The healing Pastor grabbed his ears and said a prayer. The Pastor let go and shouted, "how's your hearing now, friend? ".

Nervously and rather confused the young lad replied "I don't know, it's not till Friday."

> **Notes:** Language is a strange thing, and how in different situations different assumptions are made.

41.   Pub Lunch

It was a few years ago, and some friends and I were spending the weekend in London. For lunch we stopped off at an authentic old pub and several of my friends ordered the fish and chips for lunch. They were amazed at the value, quality and quantity of their meal, so they asked the landlord how he managed to give such a good deal in London, and could they have the recipe for the battered fish.

The landlord confessed that he bought his fish and chips from a nearby monastery hence why it was such a bargain, and so if they wanted the recipe, my friends would have to get it from the Brothers at the monastery.

Well as it was nearby, and we had time to kill, so we decided we would go and thank them personally while asking what their magic ingredients were. When one of the Brothers came to the door at the monastery, my friend cheekily asked the monk if he was the "Fish Friar" to which the Brother smartly replied, "No, I'm not the Fish Friar, I'm the Chip Monk!"

Notes: A nice little story, whereby the monk actually is funnier than my friend. Places can be changed to keep it relevant and contextual.

42. Rain and the Garden Centre

A couple of weeks ago, I was pottering around the local garden centre, when I overheard a conversation between another customer and a young member of staff.

"No, you're right, we haven't had any of that in ages" said the member of staff "and I don't know when we'll be getting any more" so the customer nodded, smiled and then left.

The manager, who was stood behind me, then walked over and started telling off the young assistant "never tell a customer we can't get them anything" he said "whatever they want we can always get on order and deliver it. Do you understand?" To which the young assistant gave a glum nod.

"So what did they want?" asked the manage, to which the reply came "What they wanted was – for some rain".

> **Notes:** A gentle reminder to get all the facts before you make yourself look stupid.

43.   Roller Coasters and Being Scared

My seven-year-old niece was thrilled when we went to Disney World together with our extended family. When at the Theme Park she headed straight for Space Mountain – the huge roller coaster, I was scared, but she wasn't and we actually ended up riding it twice and loving every minute of it.

A couple of years later we were all back again, she was now nearly 10, and again she dragged us to the Space Mountain ride. As we stood in line though, I noticed this time, she was looking rather anxious as she read the signs that warned about the ride's speed. After a few minutes she said "I don't think I want to go on it".

"Why?" I asked her. "You enjoyed this ride last time."

"I know," she replied, "but I couldn't read the warning signs and now I can!"

Notes: An example of how things change as we grow up.

44.   Salmons Do It

Salmon do it. Hummingbirds do it. Butterflies do it. Turtles do it. All these creatures, and many more: they all go home again.

Salmon find their way from the vast ocean back to whatever tiny tributary in which they were hatched. Hummingbirds fly over 6000 miles to find their nesting sites. Butterflies congregate in the same trees, generation after generation. Migrating turtles even closed down whole runways at JFK Airport in America in 2011 as they made their way back to their home ground.

The instinct to "go home" is world-wide.

> **Notes:** This first sentence would lead our audience/congregation into thinking we were going to start talking about sex, hence the relief is palpable when we say it's about going home.

45. Sat Nav Story

One of the most popular Christmas presents for adults in recent years has been the in car satellite navigation system – the sat nav! I must admit, I love my sat nav. Last Christmas my husband bought me a new one – a more deluxe version than my previous sat nav. This new one included maps for over 32 European countries – however I think one of his motives of buying it for me was so that he could borrow it when he went rallying around Europe with Club Triumph.

Sure enough, my gadget hating husband did borrow it, but rather than asking me to show him how to use it, he said it would be simple and off he went, promising me he'd drive carefully, and not speed round the mountain passes. He was unaware that I had set the safety settings, including whenever the car went over the speed limit a warning bell would sound to remind you to slow down.

On his safe return from a tour of ten countries, I asked how he had got on with the sat nav, "Fine" he replied "except I think you must have left the alarm on because a bell kept ringing every other minute."

However, he did get his revenge on me, when I was using it, I got a huge shock when it suddenly 'moo-ed' at me like a cow. He'd cunningly learnt how to change it so when I went over the speed limit I got the sound of a cow moo-ing, maybe he's more tech savy that I give him credit for.

> **Notes:** Once again, in the end the joke is on me.

46. Smuggling the Unexpected

While crossing the American-Mexican border on his bicycle, the man was stopped by the American guard who pointed to two sacks the cyclist had on his shoulders. "What's in the bags?", asked the guard. "Sand," said the cyclist. "Get them off – we'll take a look," said the guard, disbelieving him.

The cyclist did as he was told, he emptied the bags, and proving they contained nothing but sand, then promptly reloaded the bags, put them on his shoulders and continued across the border. A week later, the same thing happened. Again the guard demanded to see the two bags the cyclist was carrying, which again contained nothing but sand. This went on every week for six months, until one day the cyclist with the sand bags failed to appear.

A few days later, the guard happened to meet the cyclist in the town centre. "Say friend" the guard said to the cyclist "you sure had us crazy. We guessed you were smuggling something across the Mexican border in all that sand, but what was it. Trust me, I won't say a word to anyone one, but what is it you were smuggling?" To which the man promptly replied "What was I smuggling, hmm. It really was obvious, all you had to do was look."

"Oh come on tell me" replied the guard getting frustrated.

"Ok" replied the young man "what we were smuggling was – of course -the bicycles!"

Notes: Sometimes we miss what is obvious, looking for more in-depth reasons, ignoring what is right in front of us.

47. Temptation and Parking

A priest parked her car in a no-parking area in Nottingham because she was short of time and couldn't find a space in the car park or on the street with a meter.

Then she put a note under the windshield wiper that read: "I have driven around the city 10 times. If I don't park here, I'll miss my appointment with the Bishop. Remember from the Lord's Prayer 'Forgive us our trespasses'."

When I returned, oh, I mean when she returned, she found a ticket from the traffic warden along with this note: "I've driven round this city for 10 years. If I don't give you a ticket I'll lose my job. I remember the same prayer also said 'Lead us not into temptation'".

Hmm, well, temptation, it comes in many different forms, parking where we shouldn't, having that extra drink or slice of cake, the list is endless.

> **Notes:** Sometimes it's amusing when we 'accidentally' slip out it was ourselves in the story we are telling, and again this can be altered for your context.

48.   The Brick and the Wheelchair

A successful executive was travelling down a back street, going too fast in his new Jaguar. He was watching for children darting out from between parked cars and slowed down when he thought he saw something. As his car passed, no children appeared.

All of a sudden, a brick flew and smashed into the Jaguar's side door! He slammed on the brakes and backed the car back to the spot where the brick had been thrown. The angry driver then jumped out of the car, grabbed the nearest child and pushed him up against a parked car shouting "What was that all about and who are you? What the hell are you doing? That's a new car and that brick you threw is going to cost me a lot of money. Why did you do it?"

The young boy was apologetic. "Please, sir, please! I'm sorry but I didn't know what else to do," he pleaded. "I threw the brick because no one else would stop!"

With tears dripping down his face and off his chin, the child pointed to a spot just around a parked car.

"It's my brother," he said. "He rolled off the curb and fell out of his wheelchair and I can't lift him up." Now sobbing, the boy asked the stunned executive, "Would you please help me get him back into his wheelchair? He's hurt and he's too heavy for me."

Moved beyond words, the driver tried to swallow the rapidly swelling lump in his throat. He hurriedly lifted the boy back into the wheelchair, then took out a linen handkerchief and dabbed at the fresh scrapes and cuts.

A quick look told him everything was going to be okay. "Thank you and may God bless you," the grateful child told the stranger. Too shook up for words, the man simply watched the boy push his wheelchair-bound brother down the pavement towards their home.

It was a long, slow walk back to the Jaguar. The damage was very noticeable, but the driver never bothered to repair the dented side door. He kept the dent there to remind him of this message "Don't go through life so fast that someone has to throw a brick at you to get your attention!"

> **Notes:** You can use this moral story about time, to remind your listeners about the importance of slowing down to look at the people and circumstances around us. Otherwise, before we know it, our life will pass, and we might realize that we paid attention to the wrong things.

49. The Broken Lawn Mower

Neither my husband nor I are keen gardeners. When our lawn mower broke, I asked him to fix it, he's very practical and good at such things. After asking him on several occasions to repair it, he now thought I was nagging him, so didn't repair it on principle.

Then I thought I would make him feel guilty and repair it, so when he arrived home one day, he found me in the garden, sitting in the tall grass and snipping away at the grass with a pair of scissors. Rather than talk to me, he walked silently past me, into the house and reappeared a few minutes later with a toothbrush saying "When you finish cutting the grass, you might as well sweep the drive too!"

> **Notes:** An adaptable amusing story about never knowing what is to come. Obviously the sensible thing to do would have been to take the lawn mower and get it fixed, but that's not funny! On one occasion the iron needed fixing and I said every day it didn't work I would need to buy new clothes, the iron was quickly repaired.

50. The Damage of Gossiping

Are you a gossip? A good rule would be if you don't say it, then nobody can repeat it. French folklore offers a telling tale about gossip-makers. One such woman, a well know gossip in the town, had told so many malicious untruths about the local priest that, overcome by remorse, she begged the priest to forgive her, "Father, tell me how I can make amends."

The priest sighed, saying "Take two pillows, go to the town square and there cut the pillows open. Wave them in the air. Then come back."

The woman quickly went home, got two pillows and a knife, hastened to the square, cut the pillows open, waved them in the air and hastened back to the priest's house. "I did just what you said, Father!"

"Good." The priest smiled. "Now, to realize how much harm is done by gossip, go back to the square and collect all your feathers."

> **Notes:** A simple little story that reminds us of the damage of gossip, something children as well as adults can visualise.

51.   The Farmer, and the Old Horse

And I can't help but think back to the 6 years I spent in rural ministry in Nottinghamshire and how naïve I was to the ways of the countryside. One fine day I was driving down the rural lanes, startled by a deer coming out of the woods and accidently drove my car off the narrow road and into a shallow ditch at the side.

But God is good, and farmers are very helpful, maybe it helps if you wear a dog collar. The nearby farmer soon offered to help get my car back on the road and fetched his old blind shire horse called Benny – he was lovely. He backed Benny up, and hitched him to the rear tow bar of my car and then yelled "Pull Nellie pull", nothing happened, Benny just stood there, then he shouted "Come on pull Ranger" and nothing happened again, so this time he shouted 'Now pull Fred, pull hard" Still nothing happened, except me getting more anxious.

Then the farmer nonchalantly said, "Okay, Benny, show the youngsters how to do it, pull, and pull." Straight away Benny took a big step forward and another step and another step, soon he had pulled my car out of the ditch. I was so grateful but ask the farmer why he called his horse by the wrong name three times. The farmer said, "Oh, Benny is blind, and if he thought he was the only horse pulling he wouldn't even try".

> **Notes:** A nice story reminding us that we all have different gifts and abilities, and how empowering that those with disabilities offer to help others in their need.

52. The Farmer, the Horse and the Wake

One of the first funerals I took was for a farmer's wife, who had died in tragic circumstances. One of the horses had kicked up its back legs, striking her on the head, sadly killing her instantly.

As I spoke to people when planning the funeral, one thing became quite apparent, she had been a nagging wife, from dawn to dust she was always nagging her husband about one thing or another. The more I spoke to friends and neighbours the more I heard about her nagging tendencies.

After the funeral at the wake, I noticed how when the women offered their sympathy to the husband, now the widower, he would nod his head up and down, - to every woman. When the men came up and spoke quietly to him, he would shake his head from side to side – again for every man.

When the wake was over and all the mourners had left, I innocently asked the widower, "Why was it that you nodded your head up and down to all the women and shook your head from side to side to all the men?"

"Well," the farmer replied, "the women all said how lovely the service was and how she would have enjoyed it." I felt quite pleased with myself.

"And the men?" I asked. "Well," he replied "I was shaking my head and saying 'no' to all the men as they all kept asking the same question 'Is that horse for sale?'"

> **Notes:** Yes this story plays into the stereotypes of women nagging their husbands, but the genders could be changed, and rather than being the minister, you could be someone who attended the service instead, to keep it authentic to your context.

53. The Fisherman and the Banker

Would you like to hear a story? Well, if you are sitting comfortably, then I'll begin. An investment banker was at the end of pier at a small coastal Mexican village, when a small boat with just one fisherman docked. Inside the small boat were several large yellow fin tuna. The banker complimented the Mexican fisherman on the quality of his fish and asked how long it took to catch them.

The Mexican replied, "Only a little while".

The banker then asked why didn't he stay out longer and catch more fish? The Mexican said he had enough to support his family's immediate needs. The banker then asked, "But what do you do with the rest of your time?" The Mexican fisherman said, "I sleep late, fish a little, play with my children, take a siesta with my wife, Maria, then stroll into the village each evening where I sip wine and play guitar with my amigos. I have a full and busy life."

The banker scoffed, "I have a Masters in Business Administration and I can help you. You should spend more time fishing and with the proceeds, buy a bigger boat. With the proceeds from the bigger boat, you could buy several boats. Eventually you would have a fleet of fishing boats. Instead of selling your catch to a middleman, you would sell directly to the processor. Eventually opening your own cannery. You would control the product, processing and distribution. You would need to leave this small coastal fishing village and move to Mexico City. Then eventually New York City where you will run your expanding enterprise."

The Mexican fisherman asked, "But, how long will this all take?"

To which the banker replied, "15 to 20 years".

"But what then?" enquired the bemused fisherman. The banker laughed and said, "that's the best part, when the time is right, you would sell your company as stock to the public and become very rich, you would make millions."

"Millions...Then what?" probed the young man.

The banker said, "Then you would retire. Move to a small coastal fishing village where you would sleep late. Fish a little. Play with your grand kids. Take a siesta with your wife. Stroll to the village in the evenings where you could sip wine and play your guitar with your amigos."

> **Notes:** Sometimes wisdom does not come from gaining qualifications, but rather being content with one's life.

54.   The Good Samaritan

At a school assembly recently, I was telling the school about the Biblical story of the Good Samaritan, in which a man was beaten, robbed and left for dead. I described the situation in vivid detail to keep their attention and so the pupils could visualize the drama.

Then I asked the children, "If you saw a person lying on the roadside all wounded and bleeding, what would you do?"

It all went quiet, it seems to last for ages, then a thoughtful little girl broke the hushed silence by saying, "I think I'd throw up!"

> **Notes:** The honesty of the little girl is admirable and gives a different ending to the story than what is generally expected.

55. The Nail Shop

In preparation for our new home, I've explained to my husband that we do need to buy a few things – oh, like carpets and curtains. He doesn't do shopping, so it's been hard work. When I said how we needed to look at new domestic appliances, we agreed to meet up in the city near the department store, so I suggested we met outside the new Nail Shop that had just opened up on the corner.

Much to my surprise his face lit up "New Nail Shop" he repeated with confusion, "Yes they do nails how the customer wants them, it's all individually done" I explained, to which he happily replied "Yes we can meet at the Nail Shop".

Then I realised, inside his head he had linked it with the hardware shop and was imagining skilled craftsman and engineers hand making precision screws, nail and other haberdashery, like they used to do in the good old days, when nails were crafted and lasted, probably over a burning furnaces with the smell of sweat and hard graft.

'Oh dear' I thought, so gently explained that it wasn't that sort of nail but rather fingernails, and it wasn't men hand crafting iron and steel but rather women having their finger nails made pretty. His face dropped, the disappointment was obvious, but grumpily he agreed to meet me there as asked.

> **Notes:** Interesting how we jump to assumptions based on our own experience and world view.

56.   The Priest and the Flood

A priest lived in a house by the river, but one day the banks burst, and the house was flooded.

She prayed fervently for God's help in this crisis. As the water level rose alarmingly, the woman climbed onto the roof of the house. A boat came by "Climb aboard" called the captain. "No, I shall stay here" the priest said, "God will take care of me".

Twenty minutes later, with the waters still rising, the woman climbed onto the chimney. Another boat came by "Jump aboard" shouted the captain. "No, I shall say here" the priest replied "God will take care of me".

With the water now up to the priest's waist, a helicopter suddenly swooped down, "Quick" shouted the pilot "Climb aboard". "No, I shall stay here" she shouted "God will take care of me".

The water level continued to rise and soon the woman was swept from the chimney and drowned.

Up in heaven, the priest sought out God and complained "I thought you were going to take care of me". God said, "I sent you two boats and a helicopter – what more do you want?"

> **Notes:** I ensured the priest in the story was the same gender as myself, to make it a little more personal, and the arrogance of the priest is always an interesting dynamic.

57.   The Talkative Turtle

I'd like to tell you a traditional folk story from India. So, if you are sitting comfortably, then I shall begin. A turtle who was very talkative, once overheard the plan of two hunters, who schemed to catch turtles the very next day. The turtle turned to two cranes for help to elude the conspiracy of the hunters. The turtle devised a plan where in the cranes were to hold a long stick at each end between their beaks. Then the turtle would clasp its mouth tightly in the middle of the stick so that it could be carried away to a safe distance when the birds flew away.

The kind cranes agreed and asked the turtle to hold the stick firmly in his mouth. Then they took off, with the turtle dangling in the middle of the stick, mouth clasped firmly shut around the stick. When the birds were up high in the air with the turtle dangling between them, some people from below were awe struck about the strange sight.

They exclaimed " What clever birds! How intelligent those cranes are. What a brilliant idea to carry a turtle!" The proud turtle could not contain himself shouted out "The idea's mine!" only as he spoke he realized he had lost his grip on the stick and tumbled from above to land on the earth, and so we say 'pride comes before a fall'.

> **Notes:** A gently amusing folk tale that has great relevance in many settings.

58. The Unused Christmas Present

My husband is a practical man, and very hard to buy presents for. If he wants it, he's got it. So, one year I decided to buy him a reserved grave space in the churchyard as a Christmas gift – after all he didn't have one of those.

The next year I didn't buy him anything, when he asked me why no presents, I replied "well you haven't used last year's yet!"

I didn't expect a Christmas present the following year!

> **Notes:** Humour can normalise sad times, caution is always needed when talking with bereaved people.

59. The Wet Present

Some employees bought their boss a gift for her birthday. Before opening the gift, the boss shook the large box slightly, and noticed that it was wet in the corner. Touching her finger to the wet spot and tasting it, she asked, "A bottle of wine? It's got rather a pungent taste."

Her employees replied, "No."

Again, she touched his finger to the box and tasted the liquid. "A bottle of scotch? It has got a distinctive whiff about it."

Her employees replied again, "No."

Finally, the boss asked, "I give up. What is it?"

Her workers responded, "A puppy."

> **Notes:** I love the surprise ending to this, although would be concerned about putting a puppy in a box!

60. Three Great Kings

Taking a school assembly can always be a bit daunting, I remember in the lead up to Christmas, asking an excited group of teenagers if they could name the three great kings who have brought happiness & peace into people's lives?

To which I got the thoughtful, and maybe rather honest reply of "drin-king, eat-ing and bet-king!" It could have been worse!

> **Notes:** A short an easily adaptable little story, you can lengthen it by adding other details relevant to your context.

61. Three Priests at Conference

Three women priests, who were friends, went to their Diocese Clergy Conference and due to a mix up (hard to imagine I know!) they agreed to sharing one family room together. The conference was a little dull and after the bar closed the three priests returned to the shared room.

One priest said, "I know, to make things more interesting, let's confess our secret sins one to another. I'll start - My secret sin is I don't take time to pray for my congregation, but they think I am a prayer warrior".

"Oh dear" said the second priest then confessing, "My secret sin is that I just hate working and preparing the sermons. I copy all my sermons from the internet."

"Gosh, really?" I said, I mean the third priest said, going on she said, "I'm so excited, my secret sin is I love gossiping and I just can't wait to get out of this room!"

> **Notes:** I'm sure this could be adapted to most trades or professions; it could be at residential training rather than a conference. By making yourself into the third voice brings in an extra layer of humour.

62. Three Wise Women at Christmas

Presents, Christmas seems to be becoming dominated by the giving and receiving of presents. Lots of presents. One friend shared with me how her children start to open their presents on Christmas Eve in the evening - as there isn't enough time to open them all on Christmas Day. Hey ho, admittedly the baby Jesus did receive presents from the wise men at his birth, so I guess it's a Christian thing to do. Since the birth of email, every year I get the same joke sent to me from someone, about Jesus' presents, it goes something like…..

Instead of three wise men, if it had been three wise women...

- they would have asked for directions
- they would have been on time
- they would have assisted with the birth
- they would have cleaned the stable
- they would have brought more practical gifts (including even a casserole!)

Well, the presents given to Jesus were extremely relevant for his future kingship and the events that lay ahead of him.

> **Notes:** Of course, the Christian understanding of what the three wise men brought to the Baby Jesus is essential background to this story being relevant.

63. Top Tips for a Good Marriage

I've got a few bits of advice about marriage: -

To be happy with a man, you must understand him a lot and love him a little. To be happy with a woman, you must love her a lot and not try to understand her at all.

A woman has the last word in any argument. Anything a man says after that is the beginning of a new argument.

And there are two times when a man doesn't understand a woman - before marriage and after marriage.

Apparently a successful man is one who makes more money than his wife can spend. And a successful woman is one who can find such a man.

> **Notes:** I love this collection of one liners, and have used them at weddings and wedding blessings, they can be adapted as your context needs. And great for speeches at the Reception too.

64. Turtle and the Young Man

I'd like to share a Japanese Folktale with you, so if you are sitting comfortably, then I'll begin...

Long, long ago, some children were playing at a seaside in Japan when they found a turtle. The nasty children began to bully the turtle. But quickly, a young man came to the rescue and told them to "Stop it!" The children then went away to find something else to do.

To the young man's surprise the turtle started to talk to him, saying "I really appreciate your kindness. And I would like to invite you to come with me to a wonderful palace - right now". As soon as the young man got on the back of the turtle, he was taken to this secret palace in the sea that the turtle had talked about. When he arrived at the palace, he was very pleasantly surprised and said to the turtle, "What a beautiful place!"

The palace was indeed very beautiful, and the king of the turtles gave a feast for the young man, and he met many wonderful people. He had never seen such a good feast. He received a warm welcome there, and he was very satisfied with everything. He thought there was no other place on the planet nicer than that one, and wondered if he could stay there until he was an old man. He said to the turtle, "Thank you, I am glad to have met you."

The turtle said, "I have a present for you, I am going to give you two boxes, but you can only open one of the boxes. You must not open both. Don't forget!" "All right. I will open only one." the young man promised.

When on his own, the young man decided to open the bigger of the two boxes. To his amazement, it was full of gold nuggets. "Fantastic!" he said shouted. He now was rich young man. So, he then thought, "The other one must also be full of money." And he could not stand not opening the box, just a little couldn't do any damage he thought, so he broke his promise and opened the second box.

Well as soon as he opened the box, he instantly became an old man. His hair turned white, and his face was full of wrinkles. His looked like an old man over a hundred years. It all happened in a moment. After that he regretted what he did, he had money but knew he now only had a little time left to spend it. And all this was because he broke his promise.. "

Notes: Not the happiest of endings, but a great story if you've had people lying, falling out or breaking their promises – and not just for children either.

65.   Two Falcons

Once there was a king who received a gift of two magnificent falcons. They were peregrine falcons, the most beautiful birds he had ever seen. He gave the precious birds to his head falconer to be trained.

Months passed, and one day the head falconer informed the king that though one of the falcons was flying majestically, soaring high in the sky, the other bird had not moved from its branch since the day it had arrived. The king summoned healers and sorcerers from all the land to tend to the falcon, but no one could make the bird fly. He presented the task to the member of his court, but the next day, the king saw through the palace window that the bird had still not moved from its perch.

Having tried everything else, the king thought to himself, "Maybe I need someone more familiar with the countryside to understand the nature of this problem." So, he cried out to his court, "Go and get a farmer."

In the morning, the king was thrilled to see the falcon soaring high above the palace gardens. He said to his court, "Bring me the doer of this miracle." The court quickly located the farmer, who came and stood before the king. The king asked him, "How did you make the falcon fly?" With his head bowed, the farmer said to the king, "It was very easy, your highness. I simply cut the branch where the bird was sitting."

Notes: We are all made to fly — to realize our incredible potential as human beings. But at times we sit on our branches, clinging to the things that are familiar to us. The possibilities are endless, but for most of us, they remain undiscovered. We conform to the familiar, the comfortable, and the mundane. So, for the most part, our lives are mediocre instead of exciting, thrilling and fulfilling. Let us learn to destroy the branch of fear we cling to and free ourselves to the glory of flight!

66.   We Share Everything

I've been vegetarian for over 30 years now, and there are some things I've never eaten – a steak for instance, or duck, or veal or even scampi. And I've never had a MacDonald's burger. So, it's not all bad some might say. But a few years ago MacDonald's launch a veggie burger, so I felt the need to go sample one and support the veggie cause. While eating my veggie burger I watched the other customers, as you do, and focused on a very elderly couple there. I watched as they ordered one hamburger, one order of fries and one drink.

The old man gently unwrapped the plain hamburger and carefully cut it into two halves. Then he placed one half in front of his wife and kept the other in front of him. I was fascinated. He then went on to precisely counts out the fries. Dividing them into two piles and neatly placing one pile in front of his wife and keeping half for himself. Then he took a little a sip of the drink, then passed it over to his wife, who also then took a little a sip and then she put the cup down between them. And he began to eat his few bites of hamburger. I wasn't alone in looking on at them and thinking "That poor old couple - all they can afford is one meal for the two of them."

As the man began to eat his fries, I watched a smart young man walk over to their table. I heard him politely offers to buy another meal for the old couple. To which old man politely replied that 'they're just fine' and how they are used to sharing everything.

I couldn't help but notice the little old lady hadn't even eaten one bite. She was sat there watching her husband eat and occasionally taking turns to sip the drink. So, my feminist side got the better of me (as it sometimes does) and I got up and went over. Woman to woman I offered to buy another meal for her. To which she replied briskly "No, thank you, we are used to sharing everything."

As the old man finished, he wiped his face neatly with the napkin. I followed my urge and asked her "Why haven't you eaten a thing, why are you wait for him to eat first? What are you waiting for?"

To which she smartly replied ... "I'm waiting for the false TEETH."

Notes: The best person to laugh at in this story, is not the old couple, but myself, for going into a situation, knowing nothing about them, but thinking I know everything!

67.   What a Cow Heard

My husband has tinnitus – which means sometimes conversations are hard between us, but I'm beginning to think he's also a bit selective about what he does hear. For instance, when we were living in the quaint village of Norwell, in Nottinghamshire, in the field our garden back on to was a beautiful Angus Aberdeen cow- with long hair and brushed regularly, she was someone's pet. Then her sisters came to join her over the winter, I remember looking out of the window and Lester saying to me "What a pretty group of cows" to which I corrected "Not a group, a herd".

"Heard what?" he asked. "Herd of cows" I replied.

"Of course I've heard of cows" he snapped

"No a cow herd" I tried to explained

To which he replied before walking away shaking his head "What do I care what a cow heard?"

> **Notes:** The spoken word can differ to the written word with amusing effects, and each person may hear what they want to hear rather than what is being said – or indeed what is being meant.

68. Wi-Fi at the Funeral

It was 20 minutes before the start of a funeral for a well-known lady in the village. The church was empty, apart from her husband, sat on his own on the front pew, so I walked up to him and asked "Fred, is everything all right?"

He sighed, looked up at me and said, "I can't use this new phone, I can't get a signal".

Not what I was expecting to hear, I gently replied "Fred, it's your wife's funeral soon, have you got any questions?"

To which he quickly replied, "what's the Wi-Fi code?"

Now getting angry, I snaped "Your wife is dead", to which he replied, "is that upper or lower case?"

Notes: Jokes and stories about funerals need to be delivered sensitively, context is always important, if you know there has been a significant death recently in the group you are to address, then leave this joke out.

69. Woman and a Frog

A beautiful princess is going out for a walk when she meets a talking frog.

"I'm not really a frog", says the frog. "I've been turned into a frog by the wicked witch. Really I'm the incredibly handsome son of the local farmer. All I need is a kiss from a beautiful young woman like you and I'll turn back into the handsome farmer, and we'll get married and live happily ever after."

"Really", says the young woman, picking up the frog and putting it in her pocket, "The way things are with farming these days, I'll make far more money from a talking frog."

> **Notes:** As they say 'many a true word said in jest' – you can make this more context specific by adding in local farms or roads etc.

70. You've Got To Keep The Worms Warm

It was a bitterly cold winter's day. A man went fishing and cut a hole in the thick ice of the frozen lake. After several hours of patient, but freezing cold fishing, he hadn't caught anything. Then a young lad came along, cut his hole in the thick ice nearby and proceeded to catch fish after fish.

After an hour of this and having still not caught a singly fish, the man went over to the young lad and said "I've been here over four hours and I haven't caught one single fish. Yet you've been here for less than an hour and have caught at least ten. What's your secret?"

To which the young lad replied "Roo raf roo reep ra rurms ram"

"Sorry" said the man, "I didn't catch that".

"Roo raf roo reep ra rurms ram" he repeated.

"Sorry, I still didn't catch that, I can't understand a word you are saying". To which the young lad promptly spat out a wad of ugly brown wiggling slime into his hands and said, "You have to keep the worms warm".

> **Notes:** If you add names of known fishermen, or a nearby lake that does occasionally freeze over, it makes it so funnier, I added the name of someone who had just come back from a holiday in Iceland – after the sermon, everyone really did think it had happened on his holiday!

Additional Stories

These I felt were less funny or adaptable, but might still raise a smile, and that can be a very precious thing.

71.   £86,400

Imagine that you had a bank that credited your account each morning with £86,400. You could carry over no balance from one day to the next day. So, every night, whatever part of the amount you didn't spend during the day would be cancelled.

What would you do? Draw out every penny, every day, of course, and use it to your advantage!

Well, we all have such a bank, and its name is time. Every morning it credits us with 86,400 seconds. Every night it rules off as lost whatever of this that is left over, un-used, indeed un-spent. It carries over no balances, it allows no overdrafts. Each day it opens a new account with each of us. If we fail to use the day's deposits, the loss is ours. There is no going back. And there is no drawing against tomorrow.

> **Notes:** In a world full of busyness and material goods this highlights that the most precious thing we have is time, a little moralistic but sometimes it is good to put things in perspective.

72. Anniversary Gift

My car was getting rather old and showing its age, so I thought I could drop a few hints to my husband about buying me a new car in time for our wedding anniversary, and maybe something a little less boring and sportier.

"I'd really love something shiny that goes from 0 to 100 in about 2 seconds" I joked.

On our anniversary no new (or newer) car was to be found, but when I opened the carefully wrapped gift and I was most displeased to see a set of bathroom scales!

> **Notes:** Well the scales did go from 0 to 140 in a few seconds, but alas pounds not miles!

73. Bible - True of False Quiz

A little quiz about the Bible... let's get started....

To answer shout True or False...

The Bible is the most shoplifted book in the world.
True. What's that saying I'm not sure. About 50 bibles are stolen every minute

The Bible was written by 20 authors.
False. It was written by over 40 different authors.

The Bible was-written from three continents-Asia, Africa, Europe
True, and also written in different places like prison, islands, and when traveling.

The Bible would take someone over 100 hours to read it cover to cover. False. It's closer to about 70 hours – so what's stopping you, get on with it, it's only about three quarters of a million words.

The Bible was originally written in Greek.
True and False. The Old Testament was written in Hebrew and the New Testament generally in Greek, but now it's actually in over 6,000 languages

> **Notes:** A fun little quiz, that just reveals a few of the facts about the Bible, that are often taken for granted.

74.   Bilingual Dog

A local business was looking for office help. They put a sign in the window, stating the following: "HELP WANTED. Must be able to type, must be good with a computer and must be bilingual. We are an Equal Opportunity Employer."

A short time afterwards, a dog trotted up to the window, saw the sign and went inside. He looked at the receptionist and wagged his tail, then walked over to the sign, looked at it and whined. Getting the idea, the receptionist got the office manager. The office manager looked at the dog and was surprised, to say the least. However, the dog looked determined, so he led him into the office.

Inside, the dog jumped up on the chair and stared at the manager. The manager said, "I can't hire you. The sign says you must be able to type." The dog jumped down, went to the typewriter, and proceeded to type out a perfect letter. He took out the page and trotted over to the manager and gave it to him, then jumped back on the chair. The manager was stunned, but then told the dog, "The sign says you have to be good with a computer." The dog jumped down again and went to the computer. The dog proceeded to enter and execute a perfect program, that worked flawlessly the first time.

By this time the manager was totally dumb founded! He looked at the dog and said, "I realize that you are a very intelligent dog and have some interesting abilities. However, I still can't give you the job."

The dog jumped down and went to a copy of the sign and put his paw on the sentences that told about being an Equal Opportunity Employer. The manager said, "Yes, but the sign also says that you have to be bilingual".

The dog calmly looked at the manager and said "Meow".

Notes: A sweet little story with an amusing twist at the end of the tale or should that be 'tail'!

75. Butterfly and Helping

A kind and gentle man found a cocoon of a butterfly, he watched a small opening appearing in it. He kept watching this miracle of nature happen in front of him. For several hours the butterfly struggled to force its body through that little hole.

Then it seemed to stop making any progress. It appeared as if it had got as far as it could and it could go no further. The kind man decided to help the butterfly, so he took a pair of scissors and snipped off the remaining bit of the cocoon. The butterfly then emerged easily.

But it had a swollen body and small, shriveled wings. The man continued to watch the butterfly because he expected that, at any moment, the wings would enlarge and expand to be able to support the body, which would contract in time. Neither happened.

In fact, the butterfly spent the rest of its life crawling around with a swollen body and shriveled wings. It never was able to fly.

What the man in his kindness and haste did not understand was that the restricting cocoon and the struggle required for the butterfly to get through the tiny opening were God's way of forcing fluid from the body of the butterfly into its wings so that it would be ready for flight once it achieved its freedom from the cocoon.

> **Notes:** A little moral tale that if we don't know what we are doing, then maybe we shouldn't be doing it.

76. Children Writing Nice Things

One day a teacher asked her students to list the names of the other students in the room on two sheets of paper, leaving a space between each name. Then she told them to think of the nicest thing they could say about each of their classmates and write it down. It took the remainder of the class period to finish their assignment, and as the students left the room, each one handed in the papers.

That Saturday, the teacher wrote down the name of each student on a separate sheet of paper and listed what everyone else had said about that individual. On Monday she gave each student his or her list. Before long, the entire class was smiling. "Really?" she heard whispered. "I never knew that I meant anything to anyone!" and "I didn't know others liked me so much" were most of the comments.

No one ever mentioned those papers in class again. She never knew if they discussed them after class or with their parents, but it didn't matter. The exercise had accomplished its purpose. The students were happy with themselves and one another. That group of students moved on.

Several years later, one of the students was killed in Vietnam and his teacher attended the funeral of that special student. She had never seen a serviceman in a military coffin before. He looked so handsome, so mature. The church was packed with his friends. One by one those who loved him took a last walk by the coffin. The teacher was the last one to bless the coffin. As she stood there, one of the soldiers who acted as pallbearer came up to her. "Were you Mark's maths teacher?" he asked. She nodded saying "yes." Then he said: "Mark talked about you a lot".

After the funeral, most of Mark's former classmates went together to the wake. Mark's mother and father were there, obviously waiting to speak with his teacher. "We want to show you something" his father said, taking a wallet out of his pocket "They found this on Mark when he was killed. We thought you might recognize it".

Opening the billfold, he carefully removed two worn pieces of notebook paper that had obviously been taped, folded and refolded many times. The teacher knew without looking that the papers were the ones on which she had listed all the good things each of Mark's classmates had said about him. "Thank you so much for doing that" Mark's mother said, "As you can see, Mark treasured it".

All of Mark's former classmates started to gather around. Charlie smiled rather sheepishly and said, "I still have my list. It's in the top drawer of my desk at home". Chuck's wife said, "Chuck asked me to put his in our wedding album". "I have mine too" Marilyn said, "it's in my diary". Then Vicki, another classmate, reached into her pocketbook, took out her wallet and showed her worn and frazzled list to the group, "I carry this with me at all times" Vicki said and without batting an eyelash, she continued, "I think we all saved our lists".

That's when the teacher finally sat down and cried.

> **Notes:** A story from America, but the meaning is universal, little things can make a big difference

77.   Christmas Cracker Jokes

Keeping alive the Christmas tradition of cracker jokes, I'd like to share a couple of my favourite cracker jokes.

What do you call a man with a rabbit up his jumper? Warren.

What do you call a camel with no hump? Hump-free.

What do you call a girl with a cash register on her head? Tilly.

> **Notes:** Corny but still funny!

78.   Christmas Day Traditions

Merry Christmas... well Christmas, the birth of our Saviour Jesus Christ, over the years has developed a range of traditions that go along with the celebrations...

In Mexico has a famous Christmas Radish festival, which is one of the most unique and spectacular festivals in the world. Huge radishes are grown, but not to be eaten, as they are pumped up with all kinds of things to make them grow huge. And on the 23rd of December they hold "The Night of the Radishes" where competitions are held for nativity scenes sculptured and carved from giant radishes.

And the hiding of all brooms on Christmas Eve night is apparently a very old Norwegian tradition. In days gone by people believed witches and evil spirits come out on this night, looking for brooms to ride on, so they hid them in the safest places possible. Nowadays, Norwegians still hide their brooms, mops and brushes before going to sleep, but will sometimes sneak out of the house and fire a shotgun to scare off the witches.

But are we any better in Britain? Well, I'm sure you are all aware of the Holy Days and Fasting Days Act of 1551, which has not yet been repealed, and how it states that every citizen must attend a Christian church service on Christmas Day, - so well done everyone here, except the act goes on to say. and must not use any kind of vehicle to get to the service – you have to all walk to Church. Whoops!! I didn't!!

> **Notes:** Always interesting to learn the eccentricities of other nations, and our own too.

79. Christmas Fun Facts

In the 14th Century, the Christmas Pudding had the appearance of porridge. It was made of beef and mutton, with currants, raisins, prunes, spices, and wine. It was traditionally eaten before the Christmas celebrations went ahead.

In 1595, the Christmas Pudding was renamed the Plum Pudding, and consisted of breadcrumbs, eggs, dried fruits, and spirits. An unpopular pudding, the Puritans believed it was not a holy pudding, and should not be eaten by the followers of God.

In 1714, King George I decided it should be eaten at Christmas and would feature no meat.

A silver coin was later added to the Christmas Pudding mix, as this wouldn't taint the mixture or corrode the coin. It would be wrapped in greaseproof paper as a 'Christmas gift'. To find it, was to be seen as lucky, and it would be kept. Other party favours added would be a tiny wishbone (for luck), a silver thimble (for thrift), silver anchor charms (for safe harbour), or a ring (for future marriage and wealth).

The traditional pudding is topped with holly sprigs to bring good luck and healing properties. The brandy poured on top is set alight, to represent Jesus' love and power for humanity.

Notes: I'm sure there must be some more facts that are even odder!

80.   Christmas Stamps

I'm trying to be organised this year and not leave everything to the few days before Christmas, so yesterday I popped into the Post Office and asked the young man behind the counter if I could have 100 of the Christmasy stamps (you know the ones of the beautiful Christmas images) for cards for my friends.

"What denomination?" the polite young man asked.

"Oh," I said and after a moment's thought, enthusiastically replied "mainly Anglican but a lot of Methodist and a few URC with a handful of Baptists and just the two Roman Catholic".

The young man wasn't quite so polite when he snapped back "No I meant what denomination – first or second class"

"Oh...second class please" I meekly replied feeling rather stupid.

How easy is it to miss the message, to hear but to not understand and in the business of Christmas I feel this sort of thing happens to me all the time...

> **Notes:** Only really works in the run up to Christmas and to a Christian congregation.

81. Conrad the Cockerel

One time my husband Lester left me at home, while he and his friends did round Britain rally in their old Triumph cars, we were in the charming village of Bunny in Nottinghamshire, a local farmer knocked on the Vicarage door while he was away, asking if I'd lost a cockerel.

"'No" I replied, "we've only got hens, we haven't got a cockerel" and she explained they had found this one wandering around the village – did I want him, "No" again I replied to which she said "Don't worry, I'll get him killed" – well I felt so bad, that I heard myself saying "I'll have him – until we found his owners". And so, I went and collected the cream leg bar cockerel and brought him back – he was very happy with his 6 lady friends in our hen house and went into roost with them at night.

It was on the following day that I learnt that yes cockerels do go cock-a-doodle-doo do at dawn. Then also that they do it the whole day long, and this one was very loud. On the Monday lunch time a tired Lester returned and after lunch fell asleep. I forgot to mention about the new addition to our family and it was the following day when after breakfast he said to me "Christine, one of the hens doesn't look like the others, and it's making a dreadful noise, is it in pain?" to which I replied "Yes he doesn't look like the other, no he isn't in pain and he's not going to be laying any eggs either!"

I've learnt when my husband names an animal, if I say "that's a daft name" we can't keep them, so when he suggested this new arrival should be called 'Conrad' I agreed, and we got o have a cockerel for a few years.

> **Notes:** The things we get up to when our other half is away!

82.   Cowboy and the Snake

The devout cowboy lost his favourite Bible while he was mending fences out on the range.

Three weeks later, a snake walked up to him carrying the Bible in its mouth. The cowboy couldn't believe his eyes. He took the precious book out of the snake's mouth, raised his eyes heavenward and exclaimed, "It's a miracle!"

"Not really," said the snake. "Your name is written inside the cover."

> **Notes:** Expect the unexpected!

83. Duggy and Phil Working

I'm still getting used to living in the countryside, but I do appreciate that it is a working environment. However, one day last spring, as I drove over to Keyworth I noticed two men working in a field. The first man in the field was digging a small hole, and then immediately after him his work mate, was behind him and appears to be then filling in the same hole. Well on my way back I notice they're still doing the same thing, my curious side got the better of me, so I pulled over and went to chat with them. "Gentlemen, I'm sorry to bother you but what are you doing in this field?"

"Well, we're working, my name's Duggy and I dig the holes and over there is Phil – he fills them in" one of them answers.

"Oh" I replied "It just looks like to me that you are digging holes and Phil is filling then in straight away - seems a bit strange to me?"

"Well, if there is something wrong here, it's not our fault."

"So whose fault is it?" I asked, preparing myself remembering Duggy digs the whole and Phil fills them in.

"Well its' Micky's fault, he didn't show up today" was the blunt reply.

"So who is Micky?" I naively enquired, bracing myself thinking there was a punch line about having the micky taken out of me….

"Oh, he's the guy who sows the seed."

> **Notes:** A sweet story that can be adapted to a rural context near you, to add to the gentle humour.

84.   Farming, Giving Good Seed

Last Saturday, Mr F and I had a day out visiting my sister and lots of my family in rural Cambridgeshire and it happened to be the Village Fate that day and it had a heritage vehicle show too. As we wandered around, Mr F looked in-depth at a lot of old cars, and I got bored. With nothing else of interest, I listened to other people's conversations. Nearby there was a reporter interviewing a local farmer, who by the look of the shiny silver trophy he was holding, had just won a prize.

The reported asked the elderly farmer "So what is the secret of winning this trophy again Graham?", which Graham humbly replied "I owe it all to my neighbours" – 'how kind' I thought.

With Graham going on to say how he would always share his seed corn with neighbouring farmers, "but why" asked the young reporter. The old farmer had a smile on his face as he took a deep breath in and replied "Why sir, didn't you know? The wind picks up pollen from the ripening corn and swirls it from field to field. If my neighbours grow inferior corn, cross-pollination will steadily degrade the quality of my corn. If I am to grow good corn, I must help my neighbours grow good corn too."

What a good neighbour I thought and then I realised I'd lost Mr F so had to go find him.

> **Notes:** A gentle moral that can be woven into other stories.

85.   Football without a ball

Imagine a football team: they have a wonderful new kit – it's bright red. They have a new stadium with a fantastic 200,000 capacity. There is a wonderfully gifted grounds team - and the pitch is perfect. The team is made up of a group of gifted footballers from all over Europe and the world. Their aggregate worth is larger than the GDP of some countries. This is one gifted football club. Now imagine then that there was no football. No ball at all.

It was once said: football without a ball isn't football: it's not even a game of two halves. For all their skills and gifting, vital for a successful club, for all the money and sponsorship, without a football they might as well be putting on a fashion show!

> **Notes:** I've used this in wedding sermons and speeches because a marriage without love, well it's nothing, just like a game of football without the ball.

86.   'Get a wash, you dirty hippie'

On a Sunday evening I had left friends and making my way home walking through Nottingham City Centre. Where upon a group of about four young men started to shout things at me – "Get a wash you dirty hippie", "Go save a fox" and the main taunts as they got closer were "stop living off my taxes and do an honest day's work" and "get yourself a job, you scruffy hippie scrounger". They laughed and mocked me because of the way I looked and the assumptions they had made about my lifestyle and their superiority over me. Of course, I was distressed and upset by this incident.

The very next day my paths crossed with one of these men again. However, the context was different, wearing a smart suit and my hair tied back, the man, who had shouted at me to stop scrounging and get a job, was escorted to my desk at the JobCentre for his 'Back to Work' interview, to help him into employment after a year of being unemployed. I think the main thing that bloke learnt was never to judge a book by its cover!

Notes: This story is rather specific to my own past, rather than lying about your own past, the story can be adapted so that the moral still comes through.

87.   Hole in One

It was a bright, crisp, sunny Sunday morning in January, and the Priest, a keen golfer but had not been able played for weeks and weeks, due to the snow, wind and rain. He couldn't resist getting out again, so he phoned the curate and told her that he was feeling very poorly and that she would have to take Holy Communion that Sunday morning.

As soon as the Priest put the phone down, he picked up his much-loved golf clubs and set off out of town, to a golf course about forty miles away. This way he knew he wouldn't accidentally meet anyone he knew from his parish. Setting up on the first tee, he was alone. After all, it was Sunday morning and everyone else was in church!

At about this time, while looking down from heaven, Saint Peter leaned over to God, and exclaimed, "You're not going to let him get away with this, are you?"

God sighed, and said, "No, I guess not."

Just then the Priest hit the ball and it shot straight towards the pin. Dropping just short of it, then it rolled up and fell into the hole. It was a 420 yard hole in one!

St. Peter was astonished. He looked at God and asked, "Why did you let him do that?"

God smiled and replied, "Well, who's he going to tell?"

> **Notes:** In one parish, in my curacy, there was a splendid golf course, so they loved this. Also the dynamics of the story with me being the female curate and the priest getting the curate, his trainee to do the work, that could be adapted to other power/status situations.

88. Our Many Blessings

I'd like to read out an email I received this week. It goes like this:

If you own just one Bible, you are abundantly blessed. One-third of the world does not have access to a copy of the Bible.

If you woke up this morning with more health than illness, you are more blessed than the million who will not survive the week..

If you have never experienced the danger of battle, the loneliness of imprisonment, the agony of torture or the pangs of starvation, you are ahead of 500 million people around the world..

If you attend a church meeting without fear of harassment, arrest, torture, or death, you are more blessed that almost three billion people in the world.

If you have food in your refrigerator, clothes on your back, a roof over your head and a place to sleep, you are richer than 75% of this world.

If you have money in the bank, in your wallet, and spare change in a dish someplace, you are among the top 8% of the world's wealthiest people.

If you hold up your head with a smile on your face and are truly thankful, you are blessed because the majority can, but most do not.

If you can hold someone's hand, hug them or even touch them on the shoulder, you are blessed because you can offer God's healing touch.

If you prayed yesterday and today, you are in the minority because you believe in God's willingness to hear and answer prayer.

> **Notes:** Not funny, but very thoughtful, I don't apologise for the Christian sentences, but you can omit as you feel appropriate to your context. And I pray that these statistics will change quickly – in a positive way.

89. Making Assumptions

It was a very hot summer's day, in fact it was one of those hot and sticky days that are so uncomfortable, you can hardly bear to wear your jacket at work, and I was working at the College in Nottingham, managing all the student support areas. On this day, that was scorching hot, I had to spend it stuck in a small room with a couple of my team interviewing for a new member of staff for my department.

The next candidate arrived for his interview and seeing me in the reception area shuffling tables and chairs he proclaimed "Woman, I'm sweating like mad, quickly fetch me a glass of water before I get called in for my interview".

So, I turned to my assistant and politely asked Phil on Reception if he could get a glass of water for the gentleman, as I needed to start the interviewing.

Then, calmly, and slowly I put on my suit jacket that I'd dumped on the chair, on which was my name badge with my job title, clearing stating 'Head of Student Services'. Well, the poor bloke certainly needed his glass of water then!

> **Notes:** How often do we make assumptions, everyone does it and when we are wrong it can be so embarrassing, as for this poor chap, and no he didn't get appointed, but for other reasons.

90.   Rat Trap and Helping Others

A rat looked through a crack in the wall to see the farmer and his wife opening a package. What food might it contain? He was aghast to discover that it was a rat trap. Retreating to the farmyard the rat began to proclaim, "There is a rat trap in the house, a rat trap in the house!"

The chicken clucked and scratched and, raising her head, said, "Excuse me, Mr. Rat, I can tell this is a grave concern to you, but it is of no consequence to me. I cannot be bothered by it."

The rat ran to the pig and with a plea in his voice, said, "There is a rat trap in the house, a rat trap in the house!"

"I am so very sorry Mr. Rat," sympathized the pig, "But there is really nothing I can do but pray. Be assured you are in my prayers."

The rat turned to the cow, feeling quite desperate. "Like wow, Mr. Rat," the cow said, "A rat trap. Oh boy, like that really puts me in grave danger."

So the rat, feeling very dejected, returned to the house to face the farmer's rat trap alone. That very night a sound was heard throughout the house, like the sound of a rat trap catching its prey. The farmer's wife rushed to see what was caught. In the darkness she did not see the venomous snake whose tail the trap had caught, and the snake bit her. The farmer rushed her to the hospital.

The farmer's wife returned home from the hospital with a desperate fever. Now everyone knows you treat a fever with fresh chicken soup, so the farmer took his hatchet to the farmyard for the soup's main ingredient. His wife's sickness continued to worsen, and friends and neighbours came to sit with her around the clock. The farmer, to feed them, so he had to butcher the pig.

The farmer's wife did not get well. In fact, she died. Many people came for her funeral. So many, in fact, that the farmer had to slaughter the cow to provide enough meat for all of them to eat.

So, the next time you hear someone is facing a problem and you think it does not concern you, remember that when there is a rat trap in the house the whole farmyard is at risk.

> **Notes:** A great moral story, especially if you want people (who can't be bothered) to get on board with an idea or project.

91.   Saint Augustine on the Beach

The story is told of St Augustine of Hippo, a great philosopher and theologian. He was preoccupied with the doctrine of the Blessed Trinity. He wanted so much to understand the doctrine of one God in three persons and to be able to explain it logically.

One day he was walking along the seashore and reflecting on this matter. Suddenly, he saw a little child all alone on the shore. The child made a whole in the sand, ran to the sea with a little cup, filled her cup with sea water, ran up and emptied the cup into the hole she had made in the sand. Back and forth she went to the sea, filled her cup, and came and poured it into the hole. Augustine drew up and said to her, "Little child, what are you doing?"

She replied, "I am trying to empty the sea into this hole."

"How do you think," Augustine asked her, "that you can empty this immense sea into this tiny hole and with this tiny cup?"

She answered back, "And you, how do you suppose that with your small head you can comprehend the immensity of God?"

With that the angelic child disappeared.

> **Notes:** I use this story regularly on Trinity Sunday, (being from Skegness I often ask folk to imagine Skegness beach, that way it makes it local and gives a context!) and it can also be used when just wanting to reassure people that sometimes we can't know everything, but that's OK, as we are in good company with many theologians before us.

92. Talking on the Trinity

A few years ago, I overheard two ministers talking about preaching on Trinity Sunday, the one giving advice was informing the other that for Trinity Sunday he should invite the Bishop to preach. If the Bishop was busy then contact the Arch Deacon. Again, if they were busy to invite the Area Dean. If by chance they too were busy then to give this opportunity to a lay minister. Again, if they were busy, the minister should tell the Curate to do it.

It appears preaching on the Trinity is not that popular with ministers, with this minister giving the final bit of advice - that never talk for more than a few minutes as your bound to committee a hearsay. Well, I hope I don't do that this morning.

> **Notes:** A limited relevance to only really on Trinity Sunday, but it could be adapted to other major festivals you are preaching on. If you are blessed to have a Reader and/or Curate in your context then as you say the appropriate words, a long stare at them from the pulpit can be quite amusing!

93. The Parrot and the Burglar

A burglar broke into a vicarage, and looked around for what he could steal. Suddenly, a little voice pipes up, "I can see you, and so can Jesus!"

Startled, the burglar looked around the room. But there was no one there. So he carried on looking for things to steal.

"I can see you, and so can Jesus!" the little voice squeals.

The burglar jumped again, and took a longer look around the room, feeling confused and anxious. Over in the corner by the window, almost obscured by curtains, was a cage in which sat a parrot, who piped up again, "I can see you, and so can Jesus!"

"So, what," said the burglar laughing and much calmer, "you're only a parrot!" to which the parrot replies, "I'm a parrot, Jesus is a rottweiler!"

Notes: Expect the unexpected!

94. The Start of Advent

There once was a Czar in Russia whose name was Rudolph the Great. He was standing in his house one day with his wife. He looked out the window and saw something happening. He says to his wife, "Look dearest. It's raining."

She, being the obstinate type, responded, "I don't think so, I think you will find its actually snowing."

But Rudolph knew better. So, he says to his wife, "Let's step outside and we'll find out."

Lo and behold, they step outside and discover it was in fact rain. And so Rudolph turns to his wife and replies," I knew it was raining. After all Rudolph the Red knows rain, dear!"

> **Notes**: Context is everything, if your congregation/audience don't know the Christmas Carol 'Rudloph the Red Nose Reindeer' then they won't understand this story to it's full.

95.   The Talking Dog

A man is walking down the street when he hears a voice, "Pssst you come over here!" He looks round and can see only an old mangy greyhound.

"Yes over here!" Said the greyhound "Look at me I'm tied up here, I should be racing I won 14 races in my career you know?"

The man thought to himself "Oh wow, a talking dog, I have to have it, it will make me rich, TV appearances, cabaret bookings, film rights and so on, the money to be made is endless."

So, he goes in search of the owner. He found the owner and said, "I'd like to buy your dog, is he for sale??" The owner says, "No mate you don't want that old moth eaten thing!"

"But I do!" Insisted the man "I'll give you £1,000 pounds for him.

"Okay" said the owner "but I think you're making a big mistake!"

Handing over the money the man said "Why do you think that?"

The man replied, "Because that dog's a liar, he's never won a race in his life!"

> **Notes**: Sometimes we ignore the opportunities right in front of us and focus on the negative rather than look for the positives.

96.   The Trapped Cat

On a sunny Sunday afternoon, two dedicated church members were being good disciples, going door to door to invite people to visit their services. When they knocked on one door, it was immediately clear the woman who answered was not happy to see them.

She told them in no uncertain terms that she did not want to hear their message, and before they could say anything more, she slammed the door in their faces.

To the woman's surprise, the front door did not close; in fact, it bounced back open. She tried again, really putting her back into it, and slammed it again with the same result - the door bounced back open.

Convinced these rude Christian people were sticking their foot in her door, she reared back to give it a slam that would teach them a lesson. Just then, one of them firmly said: "Ma'am, before you do that again, you really need to move your cat."

> **Notes**: I recently adapted this story to be myself speaking as the woman who answered the door, the congregation thought it was hysterical, I have a few cats, so I'm not sure why they laughed so much at my moggie being trapped in the door! But it highlights, by making it personal, and yourself is the fool, it does make a difference.

97.   **Twins in the Womb**

I'd like to share a little story with you, a friend - who is a priest in Mansfield sent it to me, she has one 2 years old daughter and now is five months pregnant with twins.

In a mother's womb were two babies. One asked the other: "Do you believe in life after delivery?"

The other replied, "Why, of course. There has to be something after delivery. Maybe we are here to prepare ourselves for what we will be later".

"Nonsense" said the first "There is no life after delivery. What kind of life would that be?"

The second said, "I don't know, but there will be more light than here. Maybe we will walk with our legs and eat from our mouths. Maybe we will have other senses that we can't understand now."

The first replied "That's absurd. Walking is impossible. And eating with our mouths? Ridiculous! The umbilical cord supplies the nutrition and everything we need. But the umbilical cord is so short. Life after delivery is to be logically excluded."

The second baby insisted "Well I think there is something and maybe it's different that it is here. Maybe we won't need this physical cord anymore."

The first replied "Nonsenses. And moreover, if there is life, then why has no one ever come back from there? Delivery is the end of life and in life after delivery there is nothing but darkness, and silence and oblivion. It takes us nowhere."

"Well I don't know" said the second "but certainly we will meet Mother and she will take care of us."

The first baby laughed "Mother? You actually believe in Mother? That's so laughable. If Mother exists when where is she now? I don't see her, so it's only logical that she doesn't exist."

Replying to the first baby the second said "Sometimes when you are in silence and you focus and you really listen, you can hear her loving voice calling down from above, and I believe you can perceive her presence, you can feel her all around us, as we grow then I feel Mother's love grows for us, and we grow closer to her"

> **Notes**: A great story for assemblies, or family services or even at a funeral, especially if for a child or baby, hopefully it may bring some comfort at such a hard time.

98. What Happens in Heaven?

I dreamt that I went to Heaven and an angel was showing me around. We walked side-by-side inside a large workroom filled with angels. My angel guide stopped in front of the first section and said, "This is the Receiving Section. Here, all petitions to God said in prayer are received".

I looked around in this area, and it was terribly busy with so many angels sorting out petitions written on voluminous paper sheets and scraps from people all over the world. Then we moved on down a long corridor until we reached the second section.

The angel then said to me, "This is the Packaging and Delivery Section. Here, the graces and blessings the people asked for are processed and delivered to the living persons who asked for them".

I noticed again how busy it was there. There were many angels working hard at that station, since so many blessings had been requested and were being packaged for delivery to Earth.

Finally at the farthest end of the long corridor we stopped at the door of a very small station. To my great surprise, only one angel was seated there, idly doing nothing. "This is the Acknowledgment Section," my angel friend quietly admitted to me. He seemed embarrassed "How is it that? There's no work going on here?" I asked.

"So sad," the angel sighed. "After people receive the blessings that they asked for, very few send back acknowledgments".

"How does one acknowledge God's blessings?" I asked.

"Simple," the angel answered. "Just say, "Thank you God".

> **Notes**: You could extend this story by listing all the things we have to be thankful for, such as in the story 'Our Many Blessings'.

99.   What's on TV?

Being a Vicar, we do actually work more than one day a week, indeed we are doing well if we get one whole day off a week, so things around the home do slip. Arriving back from an evening meeting that had gone on far too long, I sat down next to my husband on the sofa and asked, "What's on TV?" to which I got the grumpy one word reply "Dust!"

Post Script

If you've enjoyed these stories, and indeed even laughed out loud once or twice, then you may enjoy my other books.

A Kitten's Tears and the Mischief Years

The first part of the book is a short story tells of how Florence the little, white deaf kitten became homeless. The second part contains her monthly diary entries for five years, reflecting on life at the Vicarage, wondering why she is different to the other cats and analysing the strange things happening in church.

The Diary of a Vicarage Cat

This diary has a weekly entry from feisty Florence, the deaf cat at the Vicarage, as she explores the churchyard, greets visitors by the graves and watching the dogs taking their owners for a walk too.

Books are just £5 each and are available to buy on Amazon by Moorley's Publishers, Ilkeston,

https://www.moorleys.co.uk/?s=christine+french

All profits going to Ilkeston Life Community Newspaper where the church cats have a regular monthly column.